PRAISE FOR GIL L. ROBERTSON, IV AND
WHERE DID OUR LOVE GO

"In a time of warp-speed living, Gil Robertson gives readers an "oasis of perspective" to rest in and reconnect with what we're all born to do... LOVE."

— **Victoria Rowell, actress and bestselling author**

"Gil Robertson's book is nothing less than a public service. In an era where the decline of the African-American family and the estrangement of black women from black men are real and abiding dangers, he undertakes to remind us black folk of a simple, soul-saving truth: love is, still."

— **Leonard Pitts, Jr., Pulitzer Prize-winning columnist and bestselling author**

"My husband and I so deeply believe in the power of love that it was the theme for our wedding. Love is such a precious thing in all its shapes, forms, and levels. That is what makes this collection of stories so very special."

— **Sheryl Lee Ralph, actress and bestselling author**

"Gil Robertson's latest book celebrates God's gift to all of us: true love."

— **Marva Allen, owner of Hue-Man Books**

"This is a revealing and inspiring anthology that brings together creative spirits who make you feel like an old friend or confidant. They tell the "naked truth" about their personal love lives, from the rekindling of lost or neglected love to forbidden love to heartbreak. This intimate collection is truly an excellent read for inspiration and enjoyment."

— **Gladys Smiley Bell, director of Harvey Library, Hampton University**

WHERE DID OUR LOVE GO

WHERE DID OUR LOVE GO

Love and Relationships
in the African-American Community

EDITED BY **GIL L. ROBERTSON, IV**

BOLDEN

AN AGATE IMPRINT

CHICAGO

Printed in the United States of America.

Library of Congress Cataloging-in-Publication Data

Where did our love go: love and relationships in the African-American community / edited by Gil L. Robertson IV.
    p. cm.
Includes bibliographical references and index.
Summary: "A collection of essays and personal reflections, many by major public figures and celebrities, on the topics of marriage, love, and relationships in the African-American community"--Provided by publisher.
ISBN-13: 978-1-932841-70-1 (pbk. : alk. paper)
ISBN-10: 1-932841-70-9 (pbk. : alk. paper)
ISBN-13: 978-1-57284-714-9 (ebook)
ISBN-10: 1-57284-714-X (ebook)
1. African Americans--Marriage. 2. Marriage--United States. 3. African American families. 4. African American single people. 5. Love--United States. 6. Interpersonal relations--United States. I. Robertson, Gil L.
E185.86.W438684 2013
306.8089'96073--dc23
                    2012042605

10 9 8 7 6 5 4 3 2 1

Bolden is an imprint of Agate Publishing, Inc. Bolden and Agate books are available in bulk at discount prices. For more information visit agatepublishing.com.

DEDICATION

    I would like to thank God for giving me the courage to complete this project.

    To my wonderful parents, Gil and Fannye D. Robertson, for always having my back and filling my life with their unconditional love.

    Sending love to my double Ms., for giving me your love.

TABLE OF CONTENTS

Part III: DIVORCED

FOREWORD

---•---

My LOVE Essay

I accompanied my husband, Pennsylvania Senator Vincent Hughes (who serves the city of brotherly love, Philadelphia), on a speaking engagement before a rather large college group. At the end of his speech, the audience showed their love with great enthusiasm and applause, and my husband came over to kiss and hug me.

Afterward, we spent a little time talking with the students, and then prepared to leave. After I'd stood alone for a few minutes, a young woman with inquisitive, yet sad, eyes approached me and asked, "Is love really important, Ms. Ralph? Is it really important that someone look at me the way he looks at you?"

Her words stunned me. My heart sank as I embraced her. I told her that love is always important—especially the love of oneself.

—Sheryl Lee Ralph

Sheryl Lee Ralph is a world-renowned actress, producer, and philanthropist. She is married to the Honorable Vincent Hughes, who represents the 7th District in the Pennsylvania Senate.

ACKNOWLEDGMENTS

This book has taken me on a journey that's been as vast as the highs and lows of love, but through faith, persistence, and a respect for the power of storytelling, it has all come together.

The best thing about this project is working with super-cool writers. Each of you has deeply inspired me with your unique voices and perspectives that so strongly support the vision of this project. For this, I send each of you a heartfelt thanks. Your essays deliver a powerful display of your humanity and resonate with messages that will engage and inspire many.

Big hugs and love to my longtime assistant Jeaunine Askew. Thank you for all of your hard work, persistence, and love.

Endless thanks to Michelle Gibson, Chante Lagon, Kathy Williamson, Devin Robins, Tommy Phillips, and Loren Marks for assisting me in completing this project.

Thanks to my dear friends who keep me focused, inspired, and motivated—Ava DuVernay, Gilda Squire, and Pamela Johnson! All of you mean so much to me!

A special shout-out to: Linda Kohn and Karin Turner.

Love to my family, especially Jeffrey Robertson, Yolanda Fulton, Delores Plains, and Donald Sherman.

Ms. Toya Watts is a very special lady. Thanks for giving me "the spark" that I needed to do this project.

Endless thanks go to Doug Seibold for supporting my vision. You are a great publisher who has become a trusted friend.

A love shout-out to the great team at Agate.

Big gratitude to the booksellers, librarians, and, most of all, the readers who have supported my desire to explore black life in the United States.

INTRODUCTION

SBF: The Single Black Female. Walk through any major city in the United States on a Friday or Saturday night and you will find her. She'll be either alone or with her girlfriends, but almost never, EVER with a mate. Although she has been mythicized as the ultimate sex goddess, she has also been saddled with the reputation of someone who is uncontrollable, burdensome, and without value. Regardless of socioeconomic condition, sources estimate that around 42 percent of black women between the ages of 25 and 34 are unmarried, and that the number is even higher for black women above the age of 34. The same is also true for black men, who seem to be unwilling or unable to commit, and content to play the field. It is estimated that the percentage of unmarried black men between the ages of 25 and 34 has reached more than 43 percent.

So what's going on? That's what I intended to find out.

The how and the why of relationship status among African Americans is a touchy subject. Throughout history, African Americans have met enormous challenges that have prevented, or at the very least hampered, their efforts for marital bliss. Although the institution of marriage was illegal during slavery, records show that many blacks did marry, or least cohabited as man and wife. After the abolition of slavery in the United States, marriage rituals flourished among African-American couples who sought the accompanying social and legal benefits.

Truth be told, however, prospects were bleak when it came to former slaves sustaining healthy marriages. Historically, marriage was designed as a legal and social construct that had more to do with wealth and power than with love and romance. In fact, for most of human history, marriages were little more than business transactions for the purpose of gaining or transferring resources. Obviously, marriage was an ill-suited institution for a population living in poverty. As a result of abject circumstances, many early marriages among blacks were rife with violence, abuse, and unhappiness.

Fortunately, despite all odds, black marriages have endured. For a time, they even thrived to form the foundation of the modern African-American community. But the wounds of the past are still with us, and the frequent proclamations in today's black media that black marriages are in crisis are nothing new. Black marriages have long operated in a state of crisis, and if you take a look at Negro publications from the 1930s through the 1960s, you will discover that the issue of black marriage has been a constant source of conversation.

With this history in mind, I was motivated to compile the essays that appear in this book. Marriage is essential to maintaining the vitality and character of a community, so I find it deeply unsettling that it seems to have such little value and allure for so many today, especially in the African-American community. The black marriage gap has become such an open secret that it is now a source of endless bad jokes and fodder for prime-time reality shows, such as *Basketball Wives*, the *Real Housewives of Atlanta*, etc.

Where Did Our Love Go? explores the substantial issues surrounding relationships and marital status in the African-American community. From the Baby Mama Syndrome to the more serious implications of what single-parent households will mean for future generations, this anthology's goal is to provide an in-depth discourse on the trends and issues that cause the black marriage crisis to persist with little sign of relief. This book features more than 40 essays that explain the state of modern-day relationships in the black community and touch on themes of hope, happiness, and regret. The essays are divided into three categories: Single, Married, and Divorced, each of which present a wide cross-section of perspectives that I hope will provide many healing and teachable moments.

The dream of marriage is a fundamental right for every culture and society on earth. The time is certainly long overdue for an organized and constructive dialogue on the issues of love and relationships in the African-American community. I invite you to take part.

—**Gil Robertson, IV**

PART I
SINGLE

Life Partner

At 20,
Marriage was
An afterthought.
A bridegroom
And baby blankets
Did not snap into the puzzle
Of my ambitions.
Relationships were sacrificed;
The heart was agile.

At 30,
Singlehood
Was skin to shed.
Career rooted
And heady with
THE RELATIONSHIP,
It ended.
Reeling and fragile,
I emanated
"Damaged Goods"
While battling
Singlehood
Against a pressing
Tick, tick, tick…

At 40,
I surrendered.
Singlehood
Stepped up,
Wrapped its arms
Around me,
Caressed my thighs.
It lavished

Champagne diamonds
On my wrist
And stared into
My eyes.
We brushed arms
In movie theaters
And on gondolas in Venice.
Singlehood seduced me,
And I fell in
Love.

—Tanya Gipson

Tanya Gipson is a pharmaceutical sales representative and former television anchor/reporter. She earned a degree in broadcast journalism from the University of Memphis. She often participates in poetry workshops at the Bethesda Writer's Center in Bethesda, Maryland.

CHAPTER 1

Not by Sight

GOD WOULDN'T CALL ME A LIAR IF I SAID I'M A REGULAR, third-pew Christian. Eight a.m. Sunday worship has been a fixture in my life since I was in my mother's womb, and one scripture I can quote is the command to "walk by faith, and not by sight." 2 Corinthians 5:7 is one of those verses that every minister, including mine, has used to describe our Christian walk with God here on this earth. Believe in God's plan, trust in His Word, and stand firmly on his promises. Recently, however, this verse has taken on a new meaning for me.

I guess I am what you would call a BAP: Black American Princess. Yes, I am proud to be the progeny of two physician parents, four health care professional grandparents, and a slew of talented, smart, compassionate, and wild family members. I skinned my knees and kissed boys in fancy cars on the streets of Ladera Heights in Los Angeles. Art gallery openings, as well as doubles matches at Harvard Park, peppered my formative years. So, of course I would be on track to find a loving husband, raise two kids, and be right there in the third pew at Crenshaw Church of Christ every Sunday. Eight a.m., that's right.

One small hitch—I've never actually seen that done myself. Nope, I don't really know what one family unit consisting of a father and mother, plus two children, looks like. You see, while I had a wonderful upbringing filled with amazing experiences and loving people, my parents divorced when I was four years old. Like many African-American twentysomethings, I was raised by a single mother and a single grandmother. While my father was very much in my life and in my sister's life, he lived 3,000 miles away.

Before flashes of stereotypical deadbeat dads and independent, neck-rolling mothers pop into your head, know that mine were neither of those things. Both remarried beautiful people and I had the benefit of having four parents and over a dozen grandparents. How, you ask? Well, that large number of grandparents also has its roots in divorce and remarriage. Unfortunately, successful marriage is not one of our "blessings." Harsh, yes, but honest.

As I approach 30, I find myself in a truly energizing and loving relationship with a black man who challenges me and makes me smile from the inside out. Unlike anyone else, this man is able to make me forget my plans, toss out my sense of competitiveness, and just live in the moment. When we tailgate at football games, he gives me his last hot wing, and he knows the punch lines to Martin Lawrence's *You So Crazy*, just like I do. His decisions are always well thought out, and he can be frugal even when he's splurging on a gift from Saks for me.

He has even sat beside me on the third pew at church. And oh, did he look right at home.

As we discuss the future and our thoughts about marriage, that familiar passage of scripture comes back to me: "Walk by faith, and not by sight." Sure, marriage is a walk of faith with another person. But what I cannot stop wondering about is the "not by sight" portion.

Never having seen a successful marriage go the distance, I question whether or not I can actually do it. My idea of marriage is the ultimate partnership of love and respect—someone to travel through life with and to share memories with. I want that "we're-celebrating-65-years-of-marriage" type of relationship. The "where-you-lead-I-follow" kind of bond. That "grandbaby-and-great-grandbaby" type of love. The real "'till-death-do-us-part" commitment. Pause. Am I even capable of such an endeavor?

Stanford University didn't have a course on love and marriage. Trust me, I would have majored and minored in it. My type A personality says, "Of course you can do this! Just focus." But deep down inside is where the doubt and confusion sit—in the pit of my stomach. Is long-lasting marriage still possible these days? Am I too independent to have a husband? Do I simply want to be married because the *New York Times* says that I can't? Do I just long for the shallow appearance of my family of four on the church pew? Am I just striving for another goal on my life's to-do list?

"For we walk by faith, and not by sight."

It's no surprise that I'm not alone in my questioning. According to the Pew Research Center,[1] barely half of people in the United States over the age of 18 are married. All across the United States, the population of people who should be getting married right now are choosing not to. Black, white, Asian, or otherwise, we're holding off because of school, career, or (my favorite) "until I get my six figures," as one male friend put it.

Or we're just too darn scared. A study by Cornell University and the University of Central Oklahoma found that young couples are avoiding marriage because they fear the prospect of divorce.[2]

We live in an era where relationship statuses are posted on Facebook and then mysteriously deleted, and the former lovers are unfriended. The successes and failures in our personal lives are on display. So I don't blame myself for being a little gun-shy. After all, this year I've seen more than a few friends change their statuses from "engaged" to "married" to "it's complicated," followed by complete profile extermination.

On a larger scale, the fear of failure is palpable among my cohort of accomplished peers. The stakes are high. Creating and maintaining a successful marriage isn't like closing a multimillion-dollar banking deal or penning an international bestseller. It's not just about one person, their determination, and endless all-nighters. No PowerPoint presentation or impressive web-based graphics will dress up a marriage to make it shine more brightly than it actually does. It's you and one other person, and all the unexpected happenings of life. Personally, divorce would feel like a gut-wrenching failure of epic proportions. Not only would my dreams be deferred, but also, I would feel like all the naysayers and family jinxes would be validated. For the type As like me, it's our worst nightmare: Marriage is beyond our control.

---

[1] http://pewresearch.org/pubs/2147/marriage-newly-weds-record-low
[2] http://healthland.time.com/2011/12/22/is-fear-of-divorce-keeping-people-from-getting-married/

"Beyond our control"—sounds like another one of my minister's pulpit sayings. You know, when he's right on your proverbial street and talking about all your hang-ups. In spite of the fear, the nagging doubt, and my family history of divorce, I have to relinquish control in order to "walk by faith, and not by sight." Sure, I haven't seen it, but I have faith that I will sit in that pew one day with my husband and my children, on the good days and the bad. Easier said than done, yes, but I'll simply take this journey step by step.

—**Amy Elisa Keith**

Amy Elisa Keith is an award-winning journalist who weighs in on lifestyle, interior design, travel, health, and technology. She spent five years as a staff writer for People *magazine and has freelanced for* Essence, Latina, *and* Ebony *magazines. Currently the editor of the Living section of the website Glo.msn.com, Keith graduated from Stanford University with a BA in Communication and Middle Eastern Studies and Languages. She currently lives in her native Los Angeles.*

CHAPTER 2

Key Issues

THE FIRST TIME I SAW MY FIANCÉ, MY FIRST INSTINCT WAS TO run. I was so overwhelmed by him—his almond-shaped eyes, his broad shoulders, his smile, his smell. The attraction was so strong that I had to take a step back. We met on a weekend, and played hooky from work the following Monday for our first official date. We spent the entire day together and admitted that we both felt as if we had known each other forever. Being together felt so right. My family loved him and his family loved me. During year three of our relationship, I started to feel the clock ticking. I wondered when we were going to get married. I discussed it with him, and he said it was what he wanted as well and so I waited. He proposed three years later on Thanksgiving, on bended knee in front of my sisters and his mother and stepdad. It is now six years later and we still haven't set a date.

So what's the hold up? The right time never seemed to present itself. He wanted to come to the table with certain financial benchmarks in place, although I told him there was no such thing as a perfect time to get married. And I got so tired of waiting for him that I actually stopped wanting to get married. I even stopped wearing my ring because I got tired of questions about the date. I love my fiancé, I really do, but I have to admit that I've grown conflicted when it comes to marriage. I love the idea of pledging our love and commitment in front of family and friends, but I also wonder what the point of it all is.

There are things that I once envisioned for myself in marriage—perfect home, 2.5 kids, ongoing lust—that I don't feel are as important anymore. I see them as the dreams of a naïve girl who thought she would find her Prince Charming and that everything else would fall into place. But life hasn't been a fairy tale, and I'm no princess, and my fiancé is no prince. He's a good man, but I find myself reconsidering the future of our relationship and trying to separate what I really think from what my insecurities and emotional baggage are telling me to think. I also feel that I am not alone in my ambivalence. And that brings me to one of the biggest issues in our relationship: the key to his place.

I gave him the key to my apartment three years into our relationship. To me, that act solidified where we were and where we were going as a couple. It said that I trusted him totally and that I wanted to open up my life to him fully. Three years after that I moved and again, gave him the key to my place. It seemed natural, and right, and we discussed him moving in after he took care of some things with his place.

After all this time, he has not offered me the key to his place, even though he's said it is as much mine as it is his. I've asked for it, too many times to count, and he always responds this way: "It's no big deal. I'll get you the key." We've been going through this same dance for years. I'll ask him, he says it is no problem, and then—no key. Once we were in Home Depot picking up some things for my home, and I stopped by the key department and said, "Now we can get the key." But he doesn't carry his keys on him and didn't want to walk back to the car to get them. He promised me he would get me a copy another time. Recently I gave him a deadline for getting me the key. He said he would get it to me, and then the deadline passed, and then he said he forgot it, and then he admitted that he didn't have a copy after all.

I have to admit, this key issue has done a number on my ego. The fact that I have voiced several times how important this is to me, how it hurts me not to have it, how it pains me that he doesn't make something that is so important to me a priority, has illustrated to me that we are not ready for marriage. That little piece of metal has come to represent bigger issues of trust, integrity, respect, and valuing one's partner, vital concepts that are important for a long-term relationship.

I've asked him several times what keeps him from giving me the key, and he claims that there isn't anything. In all honesty, however, his actions speak for themselves. It has become a running joke and

I bring it up at least once a week: You want to have kids? You won't even give me a key! Even though I joke about it, it's hardly funny.

Maybe the importance that I've attached to the key is freaking him out and making him resistant and stubborn. Then again, maybe that key represents more to him than he realizes. Maybe he wants to hold on to his independence a bit longer, maybe it represents the last vestige of his bachelorhood, or maybe, contrary to what he says, he is not ready to become part of a "we."

Someone told me that if I really wanted that key, I would have it. When we were at Home Depot, I could have pressed the issue but I let it go, as I've done many other times. So, now I have to wonder what my part is in all of this. Do I really want the key? Do I really want this relationship? Do I really want to get married? The key has become tangled up with other relationship questions, and I don't have a definitive answer for any of it.

Here is what I do know: He is my best friend. He is my first call in the morning and my last call at night. When something good happens I want to share it with him, and when something bad happens I want so much for him to be there. I want the best for him, even if it isn't with me. I look at him after all this time and still think he is a beautiful man, inside and out. He makes me laugh in a way that reaches down deep into my spirit. He knows me in a way that few do.

I imagine a scale. On one side is the key, and on the other side is all the meaning—all the baggage—I've ascribed to it. And, man, that baggage is heavy. So, we will deal with the baggage, issue by issue, until the scale tips on the key side. The true key to our future has yet to be created. It isn't something he can give to me, or I can give to him. It is something we need to forge together.

—**Melody Guy**

Melody Guy is the president of the editorial services firm Guy Literary, LLC. Prior to this, she ran the Strivers Row and One World imprints at Random House, Inc., and also worked at Simon & Schuster, Inc. Guy is a graduate of the University of Pennsylvania. Follow her on Twitter @ GuyLiterary or contact her at melody@guyliterary.com. She lives in New Jersey.

CHAPTER 3

Avery

May 27, 2011, 2 p.m.-ish

Avery. I met him a week ago today. He is an actor on Broadway. We had an amazing date on Sunday. He stayed the night on Wednesday. He sent me a text when he got to work and I wasn't expecting that. He said he would call me last night. He never did. I'm waiting for his call today. Waiting on another person to call. I hate that I still do this.

I need a certain amount of attention to feel secure. He wasn't very affectionate in the morning. Maybe I'm just looking for something to go wrong. I treat people good, and I expect to be treated good in return. Good can just mean a phone call. I keep looking at the clock.

On Monday he didn't call either. The next day we talked and he said it was his phone. I overreacted. Could be overreacting now. Any hint of anything less than perfect scares me. As I said, I just want a fair chance to get to know him. He said I remind him of a guy he fell in love with as a teenager, who died in a car crash.

Someone I knew recently passed away. I hope he was able to find love before he died. I hope he felt security and love for a long period of time, at some point in his 30 years. I hope Avery doesn't dislocate my heart.

May 30, 2011, 12:15 a.m.

Wow, what I have put myself through in relationships. All the self-doubt, the rejection that isn't even real.

Things have been good with Avery. On Saturday afternoon at about 5:30 p.m. we had an incredible lunch date. We talked about Broadway, dating, how his best friend said that "the writer," meaning me, was rubbing off on him, making him speak better on stage. We laughed so much as I walked him back to the theater. He stressed how much he liked me, how he could see himself in a relationship with me.

He offered to give me a tour of the show. I had been hoping he would offer. We entered through a brown stage door. To the left were some people who looked to be building staff. One of the dancers walked in and he immediately introduced me. We took the elevator up and I just couldn't believe that he was taking me to this space. This was his world.

We got off the elevator and we were backstage. Everything was black and brown. He walked me on the stage and I stood in the middle. It took my breath away to see all of the red seats, knowing in less than an hour they would be filled.

I saw the crevices in the floor, indicating what set pieces would move. He explained how the stage goes 30 feet deep. I was in awe. It was inspiring. It looked so small but I knew dreams were made on that stage.

He took me to his dressing room. It was a dark room with a red and orange tint. He showed me his wardrobe. The soft lights on the mirror of his dresser made me eyes hurt if I stared too long.

On our way out, he took me to the basement where he warms up and sometimes calls me before going on stage. This was my dream, to kiss him at his Broadway show. He leaned me up against the pale, peach, aged wall and gave me soft kisses with smiles in between. We were both nervous of anyone coming by. I could hear the echo of our kisses in the stairwell.

At the stage door, more cast members walked by. He said one of these days I can meet him after the show, which I had already imagined. He said that his cast members would look at me, giving me the eye, asking about me, and he would say, "That's my man."

When I walked away he was still looking in my direction. I waved back. I was so elated that I walked all the way from Forty-Eighth and Broadway to Fifteenth and Eighth. I played Katy Perry's "Teenage Dream" on repeat. I got a text from a friend saying, "Hey, just saw you smiling down Eighth Avenue." I laughed because I didn't realize I was beaming like that. I was high on my time with him. Like something out of a movie. We were only together one hour and forty-five minutes.

June 2, 2011, 12 a.m.-ish

Avery stayed the night. We had one of those New York City summer dates that filled the whole day. I loved walking next to him. I cherished turning a corner with him there. He said that I stop a room.

He came back to my house and commented on how attentive I was and how he has never been with someone so attentive. I believe he likes me.

I try to stay in the moment, stay in the now. Be present. He is so beautiful that I get scared. His breath, smile, slightly crooked teeth, body, how he laughs with his whole face, his tone, his love for his work. Will he be able to ride when it's not pretty?

June 7, 2011, 12:30 a.m.-ish

Last night, the teenage dream got a little real. He got some alcohol in his system and got a little ignorant. Confessional, but ignorant. Had me wait for 15 minutes outside of Madison Square Garden for a concert. He was purposely late because he wanted to avoid seeing people he thought would be there—exes.

At a party later that night with his friends, he put me on display. Asking people what they thought my racial background was. I felt like a monkey in a cage.

When outside, he babbled about "judging," and said he wasn't ready, meaning us, but that he wanted it, which scared me. We talked about it today. He apologized, especially for having his friends go around the room and shout out what they thought I was. Ugh.

I saw an obtrusive, intense side that I've never seen before. I guess the "not ready" rant was something he had built up in his head. I just like him. I want to work at it. I'm tired of it not working out. He just called.

June 14, 2011, 11:55 p.m.-ish

I penetrated Avery last night. It was beautiful. Now he wants to do me. Ugh. I'm not ready for that. Today he was a little cranky, or just off. He apologized. I went to three of his performances this week. Just supporting. I like him so much. It'll be four weeks soon. We made it 30 days and can make it more.

On Saturday, he told me his gut instinct is that we were meant to be together. I agreed and told him that I don't believe in love at first sight and I'm not in love, but this is the closest I've been to it. I want him. I want him to fall in love with me.

June 23, 2011

On Sunday, Avery and I had a moment over music. Actually he, by himself, had a fit. My God! He got so upset because I am not a fan of the same music. He apologized for his attitude but good God, it was annoying.

Avery can be very dramatic. He is a good guy, though. I'm just getting tired of the judgment—him criticizing and saying I am not as free as him or I'm so proper. But his opinion of me is like a sword that cuts both ways. In some ways it's a compliment but in other ways it's a sweeping character assessment.

June 27, 2011, 8:30 p.m.-ish

Yesterday with Avery was horrible. I can't even explain it all. I saw a terrible person. He described himself as a bitch and selfish. I would add evil, insecure, unfair, and illogical. At one point he yelled, "Don't call me insecure again, my friend, or I'm going to get really upset." It was like he wanted to argue.

He said, "You're not perfect! You're not Jesus!" I couldn't believe what he was saying. I stressed how much I adored him and how I'm not seeing anyone else. He said, "I don't know that." I was about to walk away from him until he started crying on the street. I held onto him. I tried to be understanding.

He turned into Mr. Apology again. He was stressed over work and having a moment. But it was evil. He was a different person. His face and posture looked different. At one moment I thought he would hit me.

We found a quiet street and sat on a stoop; it looked like a movie set with a curved road, two-story houses, and dim streetlamps. Fireworks exploded like bombs. He was the bomb.

I'm curious to see what the future will be. Will we get past this? Is this the real him? An insecure narcissist who will take out his rage on those who care for him?

I want a healthy relationship, not craziness. I want a partner, not a project. All of our moments have been about him and his insecurities. I pointed out to him how he has never read any of my work. He gave some excuse that he was afraid reading my work would take his feelings to the next level. Whatever that means.

He stomped on my heart and then pled for forgiveness. I hope he knows now how to do better.

June 28, 2011, 11:40 p.m.-ish

Avery was cruel, but I'm choosing to move past it. I went to his house on Tuesday and he was the person I remembered. I helped him with two auditions. He might have landed both parts and he credited me for him doing so well. Thanked me a lot, which made me feel good. However, my insecurities popped up. All that ranting about if I'm seeing anyone else, I wonder if he is. I'm always afraid they will vanish on me. Tomorrow makes six weeks.

July 2, 2011, 12:20 a.m.-ish

He landed one of the parts! I knew he would get it. And he did. He deserves it. I'm so happy for him it's as if I've been with him for years. I see big things for him and even bigger for the both of us if we are together. I know that sounds intense, but as I told my BFF, I'm not in love though I can feel myself falling for him. I see him falling for me, too. Who knew when I first looked at him that we could build something so strong? Wow... I am calling it strong. I'm in my head. Accept the good, as I tell him.

July 5, 2011

Avery and I are over. There was another blowup last night, on the fourth of July. He got ugly again. Up until that point, we had such a good time, despite some bickering and him being moody. There are so many details. His immaturity, cruelty—then he walked away from me on the street. Something I wouldn't do to him.

Eventually we got on the phone. After hours of yelling he finally calmed down. He said he might not be ready for a relationship, but that he wanted to be in one with me.

We talked today. I asked if he still wanted to do this. He said he couldn't give me a clear answer. I was floored. I had been so supportive—writing emails for him, going to shows, helping him rehearse. He can't even tell me if he wants to work on it? He admitted to taking and not giving. He whined about me judging him even though a week ago he said, "You didn't judge me. I was the one judging myself and judging you."

So 40 minutes before he was to hit the stage—because that's when he called me—I said, "Let's break up! I can't convince you that I'm not judging you. I've been treated better than this. You know you could've done better. If you think you can find someone who judges you less and is more supportive of you, then go on." All he said was, "Okay." About ten minutes later the phone rang again, but he hung up before I answered.

I'd hoped he'd fight for it more. I don't think it will be the last I'll hear from him. I really enjoyed our time together. I thought it would work. He even said, "If you talked to me the way I talked to you, I wouldn't deal with that." I gave it my all, no matter what he put on me. Maybe that was my problem.

July 6, 2011, 6:40 p.m.-ish

He called and apologized for everything. He said that he tried, but he wasn't ready (even though he said he was on our first date). He said the demise of this is his fault. He says he is in a selfish place; he needs to focus on his career or some BS. Maybe he doesn't have the tools to make either work.

Here I am, hurt again. I thought I had it right this time.

July 11, 2011, 11:30 p.m.-ish

I haven't been able to quite let go. We talked yesterday and exchanged texts today. Don't ask me why I'm still entertaining this. He'll bring me nothing but down, but the heart wants what the heart wants.

July 14, 2011, 10p.m.-ish

I tried so hard with Avery. I believed in him. I believed in us. I accepted the good. We had what I thought was a sane conversation. He brought up sex. I asked if we could both get tested. He got upset but didn't react until later, via text. He said he would never give himself to me again and that I didn't respect or trust him. Huh? A new insult.

I texted him that I couldn't believe he would say that, and if he cared anything about me he would not contact me again. I accidentally sent that text before I was ready, but maybe it was divine intervention. I was praying to let go. The man twists things around like I've never seen. He has said before that his mind plays tricks on him. I will sleep my love woes away tonight.

August 4, 2011

Letting go of Avery has been hard. I believed it would work, but he went crazy on me. I think of his crazy contradictions, like saying I could come over but that he didn't want anyone to know, that I couldn't touch him, and that I could make him dinner but he had no food or money. His words and actions made me question where we were going. His sarcasm. It hurts. I felt so confident and happy with him.

August 7, 2011, 11 p.m.-ish

I'm feeling better. I wonder if he thinks of me more than I think of him. I wonder if he misses me. I just read through the past few months of my journal. I showed him the best part of myself. I hope to never see Avery again, but I am sure I will. The universe is never that easy on me.

—Clay Cane

Clay Cane is a radio personality and award-winning journalist whose work has appeared in a variety of outlets, including The Advocate.com, theGrio.com, The Root, and BET.com. An honors graduate of Rutgers University, Cane has interviewed various celebrities, including Beyoncé Knowles, Wes Craven, Hilary Swank, Rihanna, Nicki Minaj, Spike Lee, and others. He is the host of Clay Cane Live, *a weekly call-in radio show on WWRL 1600AM. You can read more of his work at claycane.net.*

CHAPTER 4

In My Time, on My Terms

TWO DECADES BEFORE MAYA RUDOLPH AND HER ZANY CREW brought the laughs in *Bridesmaids*, I spent a lazy afternoon watching a made-for-TV movie with the same name. Though the specifics are a bit fuzzy now, I recall that the plot centered on a quartet of besties who return home for a friend's wedding. Each woman had her own personal dramas going on, but my attention was drawn to a character named Caryl. She was the single girl of the group. As soon as her backstory revealed that she was driven by her career, hence not obsessed with landing a husband, I thought: *I know her. That's going to be me.*

I'm the first to admit that I've been focused on blazing my career path, but more than anything, I'd consider myself a dreamer. As an only child, I spent a lot time daydreaming about what I wanted to do and who I wanted to be once I left the nest. Needless to say, I had many, many dreams.

My first bright idea was to be a pediatrician, but then I realized that what I actually wanted to do was care for newborns. I thought being a maternity ward nurse might be a better fit. Then I wanted to be a dancer and a model and a writer and a fashion buyer and an advertising executive, and so on, and so on. Oh, and I should also mention that I wanted to live in a different city every year, which my grandmother thought was *the* most ridiculous thing she'd ever heard. I wanted to do it all, but in none of my childhood fantasies did I ever envision myself as a "Mrs."

When I was in high school, a senior classmate of mine arrived at school, hysterical and in tears. Since graduation was soon approaching, I couldn't imagine why she was so upset. Then she told me what was going on at home. Her father had announced that he was leaving her mother, which was devastating enough. The bigger blow was that her mother had never held a job and had no means of supporting herself. My friend was even more upset by the fact that, sadly, at 18 she had more marketable skills than her mother. I was speechless. I felt terrible for her, but deep inside, I couldn't imagine how such a thing could happen. I knew I would never find myself in such a situation. Never.

I am my mother's daughter. She blessed me with her middle name and fortified me with the strength and freedom to conquer the world. She raised me by herself, from the beginning, and sacrificed to provide for me and expose me to as much as possible. She had a plan for herself, too. As a kid, I accompanied her to register for her college courses, watched as she studied at the kitchen table, and cheered her on when she walked across the stage to get her degree. She was also the head of our household and earned every dollar. My father, to whom she'd been married before I was born, wasn't in the picture, so I didn't have much of a concept of what marriage entailed. I didn't have an understanding of what it meant to share the joy and the weight of life. What I saw, what I *knew*, was that my mother did everything, so I thought that's how it worked. I also knew, at a very young age, that I would have to rely on myself. I was to be my own savior.

As much as marriage was a foreign concept to me as a young woman, I naïvely assumed that all married couples were happy. Since I'd never seen my parents together, I didn't understand how circumstances and dynamics of a marriage changed over time or how *people* changed and ultimately grew apart. I also didn't know what it took to stay united. I continued to be in the dark about such matters, even as I watched many of my friends get hitched. Just as I was focused on making my dreams come true, I believed that getting married was the final frontier for those who wanted to be married. What I later learned is that life is not so simple. I would also learn that many people—including a handful of my friends—believed that being single was a social crime.

The first time I walked down the aisle was for the wedding of a dear family friend. I think I was about seven years old and I was beyond thrilled to be the flower girl. My mother was a bridesmaid and she, along with my grandmother, made all of the dresses for the bridal party. I remember being so excited to wear baby's breath in my hair and, of course, pose for pictures. I loved the bride and groom, who are still married today, and I was so happy to be included in the festivities. Theirs was the first of many weddings in which I'd participate, but as I got older, I realized that the ceremony was just the beginning. Marriage was a completely different entity, one that would also change my relationships with my friends, and not necessarily for the better.

Over the years, I've surely done my fair share of bridesmaid duty. I've worn the standard pastel dresses and those horrid, dyed-to-match shoes with pride, and I've adorned my lobes with dainty earrings of the bride's choosing. Though I'm embarrassed to admit it, I still have a few of the dresses tucked in the back of my closet because I drank all of that Kool-Aid about being able to wear them again. Now I know that's a lie most brides tell their bridesmaids, but back then, I happily played along. I've also bought bridal shower and wedding gifts, hosted baby showers, and shipped care packages across state lines. I've celebrated my friends as their lives expanded. Ironically, sadly, what I often received in return was judgment, and even misdirected resentment. Although nobody wants to 'fess up to it, relationships get tricky when your friends get married, especially when you're single. Things change quickly and in rather excruciating ways.

There's a scene towards the end of the 2010 *Bridesmaids* movie when Maya Rudolph, as bride-to-be Lillian, asks her single bridesmaid, "Well, what about you? What's going to happen to you?" Though this bridesmaid was an utterly extreme case of nutty, I knew exactly how she felt in that moment. Having been on the receiving end of such pity, I can honestly say that it's no fun—at all. In my case, it was as though my friends were acutely aware that they'd hit the jackpot, while they looked at me as though I was stuck buying scratch-off lotto tickets. I didn't feel that way about myself, but because I wasn't on the marriage track, I was treated like I didn't measure up. To put it one way, I wasn't part of their "demo." In no time, conversations were peppered with questions like, "So, are you seeing anybody special?" and "Are you okay?" It was as if my life, my very existence, didn't count until I settled down. That was upsetting, to the say the least, and it really hurt my feelings.

After the pity came the resentment. When my married girlfriends weren't keeping tabs on my dance card, they seemed to resent what was going on in my life. Everything became a competition, which was a strange position for me to be in because I'm not a competitor. I run my own race, always have. While they were wondering why I wasn't spending my days and nights searching for a husband, I was actually using that energy to search for *myself*. Though it might sound selfish, it's something that I needed to do, on my own. I didn't think it was such a big deal, but having the time and space to focus on myself is precisely what I think many friends came to resent. It made for very uncomfortable situations.

I'll never forget when a longtime friend, who'd grown increasingly frustrated by my single status, blurted out, in mixed company, "I don't know *what* you're waiting for!" That wasn't the first of the many jabs she'd tossed my way, but it would be the last. Unfortunately, our relationship never recovered. I had another girlfriend tell me—*without* judgment, thankfully, "Sometimes, I'm happy about being 'off the market,' but then I see how *your* time really belongs to you. I miss having that." She was probably the only person to be honest with me about what *she* was going through, as opposed to turning against me, and I was happy to be able to talk it out. As for some of my other friends, it eventually became necessary to put some distance between us, just to maintain the peace. That caused pain on both sides.

Along with dealing with the ways my friendships were changing, I knew that, for the most part, society considers being single as some sort of stigma. What I didn't know, but have since learned, is that many statistics point to almost half of black women in the United States being single.

I recently saw *Something New*, which is a movie that I really enjoyed. It was shot beautifully, Blair Underwood was his usual fine, chocolate self, and I wasn't mad at Sanaa Lathan's character, Kenya, for stepping outside of her comfort zone to find love. What I didn't like so much was the national debate the film later sparked about the plight of the Single Black Female, which seemed to be the top story on almost every prime-time news magazine. That drove me crazy, mainly because I never saw myself represented. Instead, it was as if single black women were always desperate for a man and felt unworthy because they hadn't found a husband. While that might be true for some women—and my heart goes out to them, really—I was offended by the huge generalization. That's not my story. And besides, I don't consider myself to be anybody's statistic. I was, and am, just living.

As I continue on my journey, I'm trying to stay open to what life has in store. While I'm proud to have actualized a great number of items on my long list of dreams, there's still so much I want to do and so many places I want to see.

When I meet new people and they ask if I'm married, I can see the shock on their faces when I say no. The next question is always the same: "Well, do you *want* to get married?" I reply honestly: "I don't know"—and then there's an awkward pause. Recently, a friend of mine shocked me with his follow-up. "I'd love to see you get married," he said, "you deserve it." There was no edge in his voice, just love and hope and a concern for my happiness. I appreciated what he had to say and it really got me to thinking. At this juncture, perhaps it's time I consider embarking on my next, uncharted adventure—this go-round, with someone to hold my hand along the way. We'll see.

I haven't a clue how my movie will play out, but I'd like to think that I'll be content, no matter what. If, by chance, the universe is intent on me crossing paths with my match and falling head over heels, I say bring it on. Who knows? All I can do is be myself and hope for the best. But before I drive off into the sunset with the man who's been selected for me, best believe that my écru gown, gold strappies, and dangling baubles will be fabulous, and my ever-so-natural face beat and flawless—*that* much I do know!

Again, we shall see.

—**Regina Robertson**

Regina R. Robertson is West Coast editor of Essence. *Her written work has also been published in* O, Ebony, *the Associated Press newswire,* Giant, Honey, *and Venice. Robertson has been a featured guest on NPR,* The View, E!, Centric, *and the TV Guide Channel, and has been quoted in the* Los Angeles Times. *Her website is reginarobertson. com.*

CHAPTER 5

Fear to Love

FEAR. DO WE KNOW WHAT IT LOOKS LIKE? DO WE KNOW WHAT it sounds like? For me, fear is defined as: "An unpleasant emotion caused by the belief that someone or something is dangerous, likely to cause pain, or a threat." When it comes to relationships in the black community, it seems there is plenty to fear. When I speak to black people about relationships, usually the first statement I hear is something about *why* they aren't in a relationship. As a bachelor I have my own reservations about relationships, but that doesn't mean I don't want to be in one per se. However, even I am afraid: I've tabled my own relationship status out of fear of being distracted from my goals. I'm no different than most in the black community because for the most part, everyone's fears are self-imposed.

Many black singles act like, after so many failed relationships, there's no point in making the effort again. Then there are those who don't want the pain of being hurt again. These are excuses to curtail our fears. We know what excuses are, but rarely do we recognize them when we use them.

We go through so many motions because of fear. Excuses come in so many forms: *It's not the right time, he/she isn't a good fit, what will my friends think? I don't want to get hurt again, that person isn't my type, there aren't any good men/women left, the statistics say this that and the third, I don't date outside of my race, I can't commit, everyone is on the down low, I can't live with anyone else, I don't want to move, I love my job, I don't want to lose my life, I don't want to lose control, maybe I'm supposed to be single,* blah, blah, blah, so on and so forth.

I could go on, but what's the point? We make excuses when we are scared, but it's up to you to overcome your fears. Black people in particular have to work at this. Perhaps it's a remnant of slavery, but it is precisely these fears, excuses, and insecurities that can destroy what would otherwise be a happy relationship.

Most of us don't want to be alone and are dismayed at the pain of being rejected or abandoned. As black people we tend to think we can rely on faith, or our inner strength, and we honestly believe that we could survive alone but that life is better and easier with others. We fear being left due to death, rejection, illness, or physical and emotional distance; but even present-day African Americans recognize that their strength comes from their communities and their people living and working together.

Sometimes our fears make us worry that our partner will change, and other times we fear that they won't change at all. New job, more money, pregnancy, success—even good changes can be hard to deal with. When familiar habits and routines are changed, we feel a sense of unease because we have adjustments to make and new routines to create.

In the dawn of the upwardly mobile black single, change is one of the biggest threats to losing one's individual identity. If you are part of a relationship, then you share an equal responsibility for making the relationship work. You can remain an individual because you still have your own history and your own wants and needs. Don't compromise yourself to make another happy. If your partner is unable to respect who you are, and will do nothing to make the relationship work, then you need to consider the feasibility of that relationship. You have to keep your identity and respect and love your partner's identity, but you also have to let your walls down and be able to receive love too.

The Force M.D.'s once sang, "Love is a house and you got the key." That's right—communication is essential to the development of any relationship. I may be a man but I do know that speaking honestly about your feelings is the best way to deal with relationship issues. Discussing your relationship fears, hopes, and motivations, and finding practical solutions, will make fears wash away from your daily routine. Even fighting about your feelings is better than repressing or stuffing them down deep inside your tormented soul (just be respectful, please). You must talk to your partner about your fears and don't feel embarrassed. You have a genuine problem and your partner can be your unconditional guarantee of support, and he or she will be relieved to know what makes you unhappy.

While Black Love can be strong, real love is unselfish, open, and kind. To love someone, you don't have to be overinvolved, call him or her incessantly, fight for attention, or be some jealous controlling psycho stalker. It certainly doesn't help if you always have walls up. Be the partner you are looking for in your life. If you have a fear, then you have to be able to accept it and the fact that you have a problem. Once you have accepted your fear then you can deal with it, but until your mind accepts it, it can only get worse.

Many single blacks are afraid to accept love because they fear losing it. So what? A relationship might not work, that's life, that doesn't mean that your next one won't be the stuff that dreams are made of. You cannot live your life hiding away and being scared of life and love; it's an unbelievable waste and it's not a healthy way to live. In fact, it's not living at all. You have to take a chance, you have to put yourself out there, and if you can't find the courage then you end up only cheating yourself. Get over yourself and use those failed relationships as learning experiences, not excuses. Don't be afraid of what you need most—LOVE.

Use communication to get from fear to love—not just in your relationships, but also in your everyday interactions with people. Spread love. Bring back the spirit and the pride in each other that our ancestors felt. Speak to your brothers and sisters for no reason at all. You may find that you get another smile right back—maybe even a "Hello, how are you." Sometimes, all love needs is a "hello"—so don't be afraid.

—David Horton

David Horton, currently completing law school, is the bestselling author of Negro Intellect: A Guide for Young Black Males *and* Black Princess: A Guide for Young Females. *Check out his books at negropublishing.com.*

CHAPTER 6

To Swirl, or Not to Swirl?

HE WAS TALL—IMPORTANT FOR A LOT OF WOMEN, BUT FOR one who stands five feet nine, crucial—and even in her five-inch heels, he towered over her. Fine and athletic: he played pickup ball. Ooh wee—fun-neeee! He had them cracking up all night! And generous, too. He didn't let anyone else pay for one round, plus he left a *nice* tip. Gentlemanly, courteous, chivalrous. And more than one sister noted how cute he was, if we're being honest. The right age, the right kind of job, and he was *definitely* trying to holla. Everything was perfect!

Except he wasn't black.

"I don't get jiggy with the swirl," my soror said, and with that, the subject was closed.

Chocolate and vanilla, swirled in the dating world. I've often wondered why the swirl I do see seems so lopsided. The swirling I notice is black and white and the black is almost invariably male. For the longest time, I thought white men simply didn't ask out black women, and that still seems to be a large part of it. But something else is at play here.

A lot of black women just don't want to get jiggy with the swirl.

Let's be honest. For some black men—not all—the white woman is still a chest-thumping, high-water mark of achievement: "I got that." Uncle Ruckus will tell you that white women are beautiful with their thin lips and long necks, and that they smell like an angel's burp. Say what you will about the ragged remnants of slavery; Massa's insistence on protecting the precious Missus from even the glance of a studly field hand left as much of a legacy, I believe, as the n-word. Emmett Till was brutalized because he supposedly whistled at a white woman across the street. So today, these men will show *you*. They'll get the quite-willing Missus out of her knickers, and they'll dare you to say a word. They'll strut proudly in front of the crowd with an adoring Caucasian of variable attractiveness who may have her own legacy-inspired, rebellious reasons for wanting to explore a dark stud herself. People often want what they're told they shouldn't have, yes?

There are plenty of high-profile black men who are with black women and seemingly happy about it: Barack Obama, Denzel Washington, Samuel L. Jackson, Shawn "Jay-Z" Carter, Boris Kodjoe, Grant Hill. Photos of them with their wives are likely to draw fond sighs from black women, along with the Twitter-inspired hashtag #BlackLove. There are also high-profile white men happily embracing black spouses: Robert DeNiro, Robin Thicke, David Bowie— not to mention whoever's courting Halle Berry. It's not as *if all* black women say no to interracial dating. But the same history that put Massa and Missus's daughter Missy on an end-all be-all pedestal also left scars for black women. Objectified and victimized by Massa as his belly-warmer-on-demand, the black woman's sexuality was taken from her brutally in those days, as the black man stood helplessly, painfully by, lest he lose his life trying to defend her honor. Theoretically, slavery's remnants then resulted in generations of black men who either worked to protect black women's honor or who reached for Missy, the forbidden fruit.

I was stunned the first time I heard a black woman say she could never date a white man because her ancestors might have been raped during slavery. There was also shock the first time a black man told me—angrily!—that he would be appalled at a black woman dating a white man, for the same reason. A historic grudge, made modern.

I have to wonder why some men whose blackness seems so very part of, so essential to, so inescapable from what they achieve; who have made trendsetting marks upon this color-saturated world— Sammy Davis, Jr., Quincy Jones, Cornel West, Tiger Woods, Julian Bond, Sidney Poitier, Harry Belafonte—find themselves in relationships with white women. Their discourse and the barriers they broke link them so strongly to black pride that they might as well walk around wearing a royal mantle—and so, when their white spouses are revealed, the common reaction is, "Huh?!"

Then I have to wonder why I even try to look from the outside in at somebody else's relationship. Oh, I'm embarrassed to be caught on *that* judge's bench. Truth be told, in theory, I am in favor of interracial relationships. Yes. I'm absolutely *sick* of the little box you're supposed to check on this or that form that identifies your race—yet at the same time I embrace the one-drop rule because I think it shows how stupid its architects were.

I embrace the one-drop rule, by the way, because I think putting the "black" label on someone who "looks" white shows how inane the social construct of race can be to begin with. I chuckle at the white coworkers who believe our colleague is white while everyone who's black in the office thinks she's passing. I think a generation (or two or three) of mixing races will make everyone so hard to genetically identify that asking anyone to check a little box to indicate their race and ethnicity will become as stupid as the one-drop rule itself.

Yet, while I'm all rah-rah for race mixing, I still give a suspicious side-eye when I see a fine black man with a Becky on his arm. Is he one of those guys who think black women are too loud/angry/nappy headed/independent/unambitious/not good enough? Is this chick some sort of "prize" to him, or did they fall in love without regard to color?

"Cuba Gooding, Jr.," I nod, oh-so-knowingly, "that's an example of an interracial marriage that you *know* was based on love. I mean, they fell in love in high school! Not after he got rich and famous, like that basketball player or that singer dude or that wide receiver!"

Sigh.

In the mid-2000s, many sources were reporting that around 73 percent of black/white interracial relationships involved black men with white women. The 2010 Census found that black men are nearly three times as likely to marry outside the race than are black women—24 percent versus 9 percent. Interracial marriage is at an all-time high in the United States, says the Census: 1 out of every 12 marriages is mixed. A 2011 Gallup poll found that 86 percent of people in the United States approve of interracial relationships. So swirl jigginess is growing in acceptance and reality, but black women seem hesitant.

The hesitation may stem from the basic idea of Black Love and modeling our families after what we see with older generations; it may be the desire to be with someone who relates to a shared ancestry, and who can discuss Driving While Black because he "gets it." And there are many black men who feel the same way.

Let me be clear: I understand that *je ne sais quoi* about black men that makes women swoon. Not sure if it's something in the DNA or the pheromones, but there is an innate pull that is often felt in what seems to be the fiber of one's being when *that* black man comes near. Don't make me try to analyze why it's white men—the blue-eyed soul types or the silent, strong types, the ones who just *walk* like they just have that som'n som'n—who make *me* swoon. It's clear that that indefinable quality, that unspoken gasconade, may be seemingly inherent in the brothers, yet it is not relegated solely to black men. So swirling shouldn't be dominated by them, either.

Let's get jiggy with it, sisters.

—**Veronica Waters**

Veronica Waters is a news anchor and reporter for Cox Media Group in Atlanta, on News/Talk WSB, KISS 104, and B98.5 FM. She is an alumna of Alcorn State University and Mississippi State University. In 2007, the Radio Television Digitial News Association RTDNA honored her series "Snaring Internet Predators" with an Edward R. Murrow Regional Award for Investigative Reporting. Waters is a dues-paying, nine-white-pearl-wearing member of Delta Sigma Theta Sorority, Inc.

CHAPTER 7

R&B Love Letters

*"Music is a powerful tool in the form of communication
[that] can be used to assist in organizing communities."*

—Gil Scott-Heron (1979)

"Understand while you dance."

—The O'Jays (1976)

L IVING IN AN ERA IN WHICH THE SHADOW OF THE MOYNIHAN
Report (1965) loomed overhead like a dark and ominous
cloud, my mother and father—although divorced—made
a conscious decision to raise me properly through collab-
orative effort. In spite of their ill-fated marriage, I, the byproduct of
their love affair, came first above disagreements regarding the future
of worldly things (i.e., the house, the cars, other material property).
Such a narrative ran counter to the prevailing portrayal of African-
American families as dysfunctional and predestined for failure.

Similar to black families, Black Love and black music have been
falsely depicted in mainstream media outlets. Each term's connota-
tion has evolved drastically over the years, but the denotative meanings have never changed. The love of self, family, and community
still remain a large part of African-American cultural production.

I have always been in awe of Stevie Wonder. His musical genius—
so great that he became a master musician in spite of his blindness—
always captivated me. In the year of my birth, 1984, he dominated
the Billboard Hot 100 for three weeks with "I Just Called to Say I
Love You." Through a simple song with a simple theme, Wonder
captured the complex ramifications that a simple gesture can have
in the game of romance. Perhaps Wonder's blindness allowed him to
better see the complicated meanings behind such simple ideas.

The same could be said a decade later, when Boyz II Men—Michael McCary, Nathan Morris, Wanya Morris, and Shawn Stockman—soared up the very same Billboard chart in 1994. The Philadelphia quartet's "On Bended Knee" performed better than "I Just Called to Say I Love You," with six weeks in the top spot. And upon reflection, the group's stage name was incredibly fitting, because their lyrics followed their own maturation as well as taught many young boys how to become men.

Unlike my father, I was timid and shy. He had a way with words—and people—that did not come naturally to me (it was something I would struggle for years to master). Nevertheless, despite our differing personalities and countless miles between us, he inadvertently taught me the essence of cool and the basics of courting through the voice of Babyface. Unbeknownst to him, during one of his holiday visits, I stumbled upon a copy of *For the Cool in You* (1993), which I stole out of fear that I would forget Kenneth Edmonds's name and because I lacked the funds to purchase the album on my own (yikes! family history has been unearthed—but for the record, I was only nine years old). For the first time, I was introduced to a black man who defied the traditional paradigms of black masculinity. Babyface was soft-spoken and introspective; I was Babyface, and Babyface was me. I devoured his love tutorials, in particular "Never Keeping Secrets," an ode to fidelity and the importance of clear communication.

How interesting that, in the midst of social and political discourse on the absence or sheer incompetence of African-American fathers and marital partners, two countering sonic images reigned supreme in America's public consciousness over the span of a decade—by African American men openly communicating and stepping up to their responsibilities, no less!

Changes in technology, business, artists, and consumer habits have shifted how Black Love is expressed in music. In 2003, the National Academy of Recording Arts and Sciences seemed to be confused about, though at least aware of, the changing times when they introduced a new category to its Grammy Awards: Contemporary R&B. The key differences between "regular" R&B and Contemporary R&B: musical production, vocal arrangements, and youthful artists fond or familiar with rap music.

Concerned with the music that began taking over the airwaves, my mind began to flutter. If the message is in our music, and the music is the conduit for the message, then I believe that we as a community should be more proactive in making sure that the music reflected the unspoken thoughts and feelings that we keep in our hearts.

By 2004, a decade after their album *II*'s multiplatinum success, Boyz II Men had been replaced by R. Kelly, Usher, and a host of similar artists. Male vocal groups were completely erased from the R&B scene. As a result, how Black Love and romantic relationships were expressed through music (the words, phrases, signs, and symbols) changed significantly. A close inspection of R. Kelly's catalog will show that he was a staunch proponent of love in its many forms: self-love in "I Believe I Can Fly" (1996); sexual politics in "Bump N' Grind" (1994); the courting process in "I'm A Flirt" (2007); sex itself in "Ignition" (2003); and the consequences of sex in "Half on a Baby" (1998). All of these songs work on a metaphorical level; ironically, though R. Kelly wrote numerous literal compositions, they were mostly performed by other R&B singers, both male and female: "How Many Ways," by Toni Braxton (1994); "You Are Not Alone," by Michael Jackson (1995); "Let's Get the Mood Right," by Johnny Gill (1996); and "Share My World," by Mary J. Blige (1997). And the list—*literally*—goes on and on and on.

With the rise and preponderance of digital technology and the music video format, Usher stepped in with raw talent and undeniable sex appeal. In this brave new world of music, innate musical skill was no longer the ultimate factor for obtaining recognition or success, but rather, which artist incorporated the best new music technology. As I think about my favorite male R&B artists, from Luther Vandross and Gerald Levert to Brian McKnight and Babyface, their chances of survival may have been pretty grim today (which makes me sad). Thankfully, before this shift in popular music, I gained many insights on love and happiness through the original R&B, which fostered my personal growth and development as a teenager and through my early twenties.

As the old adage goes, you can't love someone else if you do not love yourself. The soundtrack to *Jason's Lyric* (1994) gave me the perfect anthem to guide my outlook on life and boost my self-perception: "You Will Know." The chorus of the Black Men United collaboration—which featured a laundry list of superstars from D'Angelo to Joe—stated emphatically: "Your dreams ain't easy/ Stand up tall and don't you fall." As I made the awkward transition between the prepubescent and adolescent stages of my life, I learned to love myself through and through, body and soul.

Around the same time, one of Dr. John Gray's books was all the rage: the *New York Times* bestselling *Men Are from Mars, Women Are from Venus* (1993). With this conceit emblazoned in my mind, the perspective of women—and their domination of the late-'90s music scene—allowed me to better acquaint myself with the other sex. Janet Jackson's album *Velvet Rope* (1997) changed my life and cemented my appreciation for her visionary artistry. Her provocative track, "What About," is an unflinching look at domestic violence. Singing as though she is confronting her abuser, Janet sings several reflective questions in the chorus, including, "What about the times you said no one would want me?" At that time I had never been in a "real" relationship, but Janet's dynamic performances of "What About," both during her Velvet Rope Tour and at VH1's 1998 Fashion Awards telecast, gave me insight on how to treat the future love of my life. As Ms. Jackson's most introspective album to date, *Velvet Rope* is a musical manual that both informs men how not to behave and defines the warning signs that women should avoid in a relationship.

As I approached my 25th birthday, Brian McKnight was turning 40. Without a doubt, his music served as the backdrop of my young adult life. My favorite McKnight album is 2003's terribly underrated *U-Turn*. If Janet Jackson's "What About" provided insight into the things that tend to go wrong in a love affair, then Brian McKnight's "So Sorry" taught me how to go about righting those wrongs, even if my actions can't salvage the relationship. A rare showcase of male sensitivity and acknowledgement of personal fault, McKnight croons: "For anything that I might've done/I apologize to you." Undoubtedly, these words will spill out of my mouth at some time in my romantic life; thankfully, McKnight provided me with a heartfelt and eloquent way to express my regret.

Upon reflection, the changes in the music industry from 1984 to 2009 (the years of my birth and my "quarter-life" marker, respectively) include: the fragmentation of the R&B genre, a rapid rise in black men being portrayed as hypersexual beings by mainstream media, and the death of the traditional album as a way to sell and market songs. It suffices to say that had Stevie Wonder emerged with his hit "I Just Called to Say I Love You" today, he would be considered too "soft" in the contemporary marketplace. Tragic, no?

Without question, a lot of this change in the music industry is due to the advent of music videos and the rapid advancement of technology. R&B's influx of sonic "quickies," while related in part to sensual imagery, were also fostered at a time in which digital platforms were snapping at the album's metaphorical heels. With the contemporary music landscape shifting under on the genre's feat, perhaps too many artists relied upon a tried-and-true business mantra: "sex sells." Maybe? Maybe not.

If verses are words, and songs are sentences, then albums embody a sort of love letter from the artist directly to his or her listening (and now viewing) audience. The enduring presence of John Legend and the triumphant return of Maxwell give me hope that positive images of Black Love and passionate R&B love letters will endure. It is this hope that directs the spending of my limited dollars and cents. This hope strengthens my love of, and my faith in, R&B music, which continues to nourish my personal growth and development.

—**Clayton Perry**

Though he is an educator by profession, Clayton Perry's brief career in music journalism has led him down an unprecedented path. Perry conducted 200 celebrity interviews between 2008 and 2012 through guerrilla marketing and "old-fashioned" networking. Among the impressive list: Clive Davis, Kenneth Gamble, John Legend, and Adele.

CHAPTER 8

Being My Own Warrior

I T TOOK ME A MINUTE TO GET HERE, BUT I AM REALLY comfortable in my skin and in every facet of my life. For so long, I wanted a relationship, like so many African-American women do. I always made my life open to the person I was dating, whether it was emotionally or literally opening up my home. I also made it a priority with my partners to have a relationship with God, which I believe would help us develop further as a team.

However, what I realized is that I was always dating the same guy. He and I would date and have a really good time, but when it came to "it," I was the person who wanted to focus and try and be in the relationship for the long haul. The "ride or die" person was always me and I would soon find out that the man I would be dating loved me much as he could, but couldn't stick and stay. When stuff came up, he was fighting just like I was fighting, but he was more like, "Well this ain't working, so I'm gonna holla at you," or, "I'm gonna call you later and I'll leave and come back when the dust's settled."

Now I am at a point in my life where I've flipped, in a way. I am not open to opening up my life right now. I am enjoying the process of doing whatever I want to do, whenever I want to do it. I like the fact that ain't nobody really checking for me like that. If you call me, it's great, but at the moment, I am not looking for a date on Friday night. I am so, so comfortable with leaving work, spending time with my dog, cleaning up my house, and taking an extra-long bath with some bubbles in it, wine on the side, and listening to some good music. That's a great night for me and I might do that on Saturday and Sunday, go to work on Monday, refreshed to do it all over again—as long as I want to do it. That's my life now. And I feel because I am in this place, whatever God allows or wants to bring into my life will be clearer for me to see.

It wasn't an easy process for me to get to this place, but I did it by looking at myself. Although each one of the men I dated was different on the outside, they still had the same blueprint. They treated me well, but only loved me to a point and were not the warriors I wanted them to be. So I stopped. I just stopped.

I did not have examples of loving relationships in my family. My grandmother, my aunt, and my mother were all married at some point, and each of those relationships dissolved. My father was at home but the relationship was tumultuous and offered me no blueprint for what a healthy black male/female relationship could look like. It wasn't until I met a boy when I was 16 that I ultimately saw healthy love between a man and woman. The way he was with his mother, and the way his mother and his father related to one another, became my example. He put up parameters for how a man should treat me. If we walked to a building, and even if I got to the door before him, he would tell me, "You never touch a door, even if you have to just stand there until I get there." Don't get me wrong, my mother taught me things that men are supposed to do, but this boyfriend of mine took it to another level.

I think black relationships aren't working because we live in a world where black men have truly bought into that myth that there are 20 women to every man. They believe that if Girl #1 won't do it, then Girl #10 will do it, or they can keep trying up to Girl #20, or whatever. There is no investment in sticking and staying. Everybody thinks it's easier to throw his or her hands up and walk away. Today, people don't want to get hurt, or take their time, when it's just as easy if not easier to find a new relationship. And then that relationship doesn't work out and they can just go find someone else, and so on.

I think there are also those men who get married and stick to that relationship, but if the marriage fails, they just decide to give up. They don't want to be hurt in that way again and even though we women like to claim that we are the ones who get hurt, men get hurt too. When men get hurt, they handle their hurt in a completely different way. Women, by and large, will take the time to go through the process of figuring out what went wrong, but men will lick their wounds for a few days and then just go out with another chick.

We all want to be coupled up, but there has to be something in you that says, "I am okay. I am beautiful. I am strong by myself," so when you find somebody, you shine even brighter. You can't need somebody else to tell you that you are gonna be okay. You have to be the one to tell yourself that you are gonna be okay, with or without someone else.

When it comes to settling down, men also have the added benefit of doing it when they are 45, 55, or 65. They don't have the pressure of a ticking biological clock. I personally refuse to allow that to dictate my timeline. Like a man, I believe that when it's time, he will be there. If it happens at 55, then that's when it will happen. Women put a lot of pressure on themselves about getting married, but men don't. They just go with it and believe that there will always be women around, and they are right.

As a television personality in Atlanta, I was very open about dealing with cancer five years ago. It was this episode in my life that helped me understand what I needed in a relationship, because I was neither that strong nor that smart to get to this place on my own.

I was having a really difficult time getting over the fact that the relationship I was in during that time ended. I'd reached the age of 36 and had finally found a man who could teach me about the miracle of unconditional love. He loved me when I was baldheaded, fat, when I didn't smell too good, had breath that wasn't that great, and didn't look pretty—and yet he loved me all the same. That breakup was very hard for me to move beyond and I cried every single day for a year and half, complaining and mourning. It was a loss that was so deep that I could only express it in tears. I recognized that I had never known unconditional love before. It was very hard to let him go because I knew what I had lost.

Later, though I knew he had moved on and was in a relationship and I was beginning to move on in a relationship of my own, I saw a picture of him and his girlfriend, and it broke me down. I took a walk with my dog and I said, "God, I need to have a conversation with you." I needed to figure out why, though I was in another relationship, I could still be a wreck about him. In the midst of me having this conversation with God, I heard Him say to me,

Who, when you were sick, who delivered you from it? Who, when you couldn't walk up two steps, made it possible for you to now run? Did your ex-boyfriend do that for you? Now, you can look at yourself and not see any remnants of cancer. Did your ex-boyfriend do that for you? If your ex-boyfriend didn't do any of that for you and I delivered him to you and took him away, I can do *anything*. If I can restore you from the brink of death, I can do *anything*. I can bring you another man and I can take him out of your life, and I can make you fine by yourself.

Since then, I have not cried a day in my life over that failed relationship or anything else. That was a turning point for me, when I realized that whether I am in a relationship or not, if I leave this earth and I am not married with 2.5 kids and a dog and whatever, I am fine and fabulous being JaQuitta. I am JaQuitta Williams because God made me beautiful and gifted. There may be other women who look like me, but there is no other woman who is just like me, and that is good enough. Whatever trials happens in my life, whatever man comes or stays away, I know that God will bring people in my life or remove them because that's what God does. There will never be a person who can deliver me from what God delivered me from, and because of that I'm good.

I realized that my marriage is with God. My love and all that goes with it is with God, and whomever He presents to me, to go through this life on this earth with me, is a bonus. I know that no person can ever do for me what God does for me, so why am I tripping? And suddenly that fear and trepidation stopped. It just stopped.

My advice is that people would be better served if they stopped looking to other people and things for satisfaction, because they already have all that they need within themselves. When I think about Whitney Houston, it proves to me that it doesn't matter if you have $2 million or $2. You can have money and fame, but if something within you is broken or wounded, it will never get fixed if you don't take the time to do it on your own. I think we all need to take the time, be uncomfortable, and say, "You know what, I am not going out, I'm not drinking, I'm not hanging with friends. I am going to take whatever time it takes—a month, a year, three years—to work on myself." Make sure there are no distractions. Pledge to yourself, "I am not going to be in a relationship right now, because being in a relationship won't give me the opportunity to fix whatever I need to fix." Nobody else can do that for you.

—JaQuitta Williams

JaQuitta Williams is an award-winning news anchor for WXIA in Atlanta.

CHAPTER 9

Wifeless + Childless = Scandalous

A FRIEND FROM COLLEGE SAID IT BEST ON FACEBOOK: "Facebook helps you remember so many parts of your life you had long since forgotten… unfortunately it includes the parts and people you had forgotten for good reason."

Let the church say *amen*.

Facebook is my social networking weapon of choice. The unintended consequences include helping remind me (and others) of all my foibles, insecurities, and questionable past behavior.

I suspect… no, I *know* I'm not alone in that regard.

Some memories are best left buried in the far reaches of the subconscious. There is something invaluable in an imperfect memory. Social networking has managed to circumnavigate what was arguably our best emotional defense. There are certain moments I do not wish to relive, much less re-read through social media. There are some pictures I'd rather not see tagged, and people from whom I'd rather not receive a friend request. I wish I had a witness. Somebody out there knows what I'm talking about.

I never, ever wanted to tell any of this story. Not to readers of my column, not to friends, and especially not to family. There is no desire to remember or recount the numerous heartaches and heartbreaks, irrespective of blame. I wasn't born with a Control+Alt+Delete function, though it sho' nuff would have been nice.

Reset, reboot… call it what you want.

Memories of the women I thought I could… no, *would* marry, who ultimately thought dalliances with my friends, neighbors, or coworkers were reasonable options. The years 1996 to 2004 are a blur, replete with hazy, nonspecific details. And you know what, I'm good with that.

I'd rather not detail how failed relationships subsequently led to years of emotionally destructive and sexually dangerous behavior with far too many women. These weren't my finest moments by any stretch of the imagination. In retrospect, I now understand it for what it was: an effort to make up for the pain, which in my mind was thrust upon me by serial monogamy. I disrespected too many women and myself as I swung the pendulum from one extreme to the other.

The list was long and I'm in no way proud.

And come to think of it, I don't even want to discuss how coming to Jesus, changing my ways, and renewing my respect for women ultimately led to my rumormonger of a pastor blithely telling the rest of my congregation that I was gay. Yes, being unmarried and not in the company of countless, random women… somehow now meant I was *gay*. Not trying to chop down every woman in the congregation (as my pastor did) was tantamount to being gay. If that makes any sense to anyone out there, please explain it to me. I couldn't win for losing. Insert the obligatory SMH wherever you see fit.

Oh, the irony.

Monogamy and respect for women had gotten me again.

Damned if I do (her), damned if I don't (do her).

To be clear, I'm not suggesting I was up for Martyr of the Year or that I was remotely saintly in my behavior. Hopefully my words will ring familiar to someone traveling along a similar path, helping make some sense out of the seeming nonsense. To do so, the backstory must be included. It speaks to the warped values our community espouses about love and sexuality, and our misguided notion of healthy relationships.

Our African American community gleefully promulgates these misconceptions through social media, at our jobs and in our church pews, even in the privacy of our homes. We keep lying to ourselves and to one another about the role and importance of marriage, dealing with it only as a social construct and not a spiritual union. This, in part, is why I'm an asshole to this day; I'm tired of being negatively defined through the adjectives of "wifeless" and "childless."

This is the bizarro world in which I live. Welcome to my AA (Assholes Anonymous).

"Hi everyone, my name is Morris and I'm an unmarried asshole."

Not everyone wins the lottery, not everyone lives to be 100, and to the matter at hand, not everyone gets married. And you know what, I'm good with that. Fewer games, less drama, and no ugly divorce.

Just be glad for me. Yes, Mommy, that *was* directed at you specifically. Just be glad for me.

Don't get me wrong. I *could* have gotten married. In fact, I presumably still could. Up until now, it just would not have been to the right woman or for the right reasons. I am sure those women probably and justifiably say the same in regards to me. I'm quite clear about my inadequacies and deficiencies, and am in no way deluded. Mo'Kelly has issues, you can best believe. But marriage for the sake of marriage… not happening.

It's about the person, the fit. We live in a reality TV world that places more value on televising a celebrity-attended ceremony than the sanctity of matrimony. My African American community has eschewed traditional marriage for Baby Mamas and Daddies, giving the side-eye to those of us men who are childless.

Where do I fit in all of that? How could I possibly fit?

Somebody out there should say amen, because you too know the feeling.

Now for the irony: I still think of myself as a romantic of sorts. I believe in love, love at first sight, and soul mates. I prefer first kisses, last dances, and holding hands in the time between the aforementioned. My vote will always be for having loved and lost, despite how painful the loss may eventually be. Yes, it seems contradictory but really it's not. I'm just complicated and my emotions are equally complex.

I believe in love *and* marriage. I also happen to believe I may not be suited for either, having been born at the wrong time on the wrong planet. Just take my word for it. I took a wrong turn somewhere in 1969 and ended up here, spending much of my existence trying to find my way back.

I know there's somebody out there who knows what I mean. We

need to band together, build a spaceship, and find our way home or a homing beacon so our people can come get us.

At the same time, though I was born in the 20th century, I've never been bound by 20th-century thinking. People should love and do so without hesitation, reservation, or limitation. That is why I've never thought negatively of interracial or even homosexual relationships. We have so little time to find someone who makes us happy in the midst of the confusion and chaotic consciousness we call life. My first real girlfriend, Evy, was white (still is, actually) and will always be one of my best friends. I don't believe in love limitations. This anthology may be about love in the African-American community, but if we are going to tell the truth, then let's be committed to doing so.

Do you. Everyone deserves to be loved, fully and faithfully. Time's a wastin'.

Do you. The rest of us need to get out of the way. That's the only preaching you'll ever get from me on this subject. The rest is between you and the Lord. Today I seek only to sweep around my own front porch.

Life and love are also all about timing.

Maybe if I hadn't been thrust into the Torrance Unified School District as one of its first black males back in 1973, my dating/love life would have evolved differently. Maybe if I didn't stop for gas on this occasion or that one, my love life could have evolved differently. Maybe if she didn't cheat on me or if I weren't such a jerk to her... Maybe if I were born at the right time in history on the right planet, things might have been different.

Maybe... maybe... and more maybes.

"For those who may have arrived late...my name is Morris and I'm an unmarried asshole."

One born at the wrong time on the wrong planet, seeking desperately to find his way back home. Mo'Kelly phone home.

I'm part of an increasing body of African Americans who don't equate life fulfillment with the institution of marriage. The world will not end if I (and those like me) don't find that special someone with whom to share the golden years. I'm cool with that.

Just be glad for me.

There once was a time when people got married in their early 20s and families had a single breadwinner who worked for the same company for 40 years.

Not anymore and never again. Times have changed and the world keeps on spinning.

We now live in a world where, sources say, close to three-quarters of all African-American children are born out of wedlock. It's a statistic often used to hatefully malign and demonize black people, but nevertheless still relevant. It signifies and quantifies the sea change and the de-emphasis of marriage for many and varied reasons.

My old-school values are completely out of step with this new-school world. My Al Green spirit of "Love and Happiness" doesn't mesh with the Chris Brown "Take You Down" new-school foolishness.

I believe in values, standards, and a logical progression relating to both. No, not claiming to be sinless, remember my backstory. At the same time, I do seek more than the lowest common denominator. The world around me says there's something wrong with being wifeless and childless in my 40s. There seemingly is no place for a heterosexual black man *without* three Baby Mamas and/or a divorce on his résumé, or both. How in the hell did we get to this point?

Growing up, I didn't fit in with the white students who made up 99 percent of the Torrance School District. Being called "nigger" the first day of kindergarten pretty much set the tone moving forward. I didn't fit in with my multicultural neighborhood, which frowned upon smart, black boys who spoke "proper" English. The white girls at school *couldn't* date me and the black girls in my neighborhood *wouldn't* date me. Or maybe it was the other way around or even a little bit of both. Who knows? Either way, I must have been born at the wrong time on the wrong planet. Life and love are inextricably linked to good timing. Of which I haven't any.

What I am sure of is that all of these things have led to my "assholeness," who I am today.

I don't fit. That's it, in a nutshell.

I was born at the wrong time, on the wrong planet and the dissonance plays itself out in all sorts of ways. I've also come to learn that I'm not alone in this regard. Dozens of my friends and contemporaries find themselves feeling the same way. Many of my generation have struggled with this disconnect, some like me eventually making their peace with it. Not everything is for everyone. There are some people better off not tasked with the responsibility of raising children, some better off unmarried.

Guilty on both counts.

There is a reason why there is so much wisdom in the phrase "I can do bad all by myself." It's because it's true.

And now for more irony.

Over the years, I've received more than just one phone call from exes offering either an apology or looking for some sort of absolution for past sins from years ago. It's neither flattering nor helpful. It's like foreign currency, money I can't spend. I needed it back then, not now. Again, bad timing. Throwing a touchdown pass a decade after the game ends doesn't change the final score of the game.

There must have been some mistake. Somebody upstairs messed up my paperwork. This is not my planet. Somebody please help me power up either the flux capacitor and/or fix the Millennium Falcon's hyper drive.

In the meantime, just be glad for me and know that although I may not be the one for marriage, I am still pulling for the rest of you.

—Morris O'Kelly

Morris W. O'Kelly (Mo'Kelly) is the author of the syndicated socio-political and entertainment column The Mo'Kelly Report, *the American political correspondent for BBC Radio and Television, and the host of the KFI AM640 radio program,* The Mo'Kelly Show.

CHAPTER 10

———•———

The Appointed Time

IKE MANY BLACK WOMEN IN AMERICA, I HAVE NEVER BEEN married. I'm not single because I believe all men are dogs, or are on the down low, or that the good ones are already taken. I'm not single because I'm too independent, or not attracted to men, or think I'm too good for these men out here. And it's not because I think life is too short to be tied down to one man, or I don't know how to let a man be a man, or because I can do bad all by myself.

I'm single because it is not yet my time to be married—a reason that's simple and complex all at once. In Ecclesiastes 3:1 it is written, "To everything *there is* a season, a time for every purpose under heaven." There's a moment when it is right and opportune for something to occur: its appointed time. Just like it takes 9 months for an embryo to fully develop, and it took more than 200 years before the United States was ready to elect a black president.

I have observed the truth of God's timing in my own life as well, and the Bible is full of still more examples. Those of us who believe know that God's timing is quite often different from our personal timetables. It isn't swayed by the fact that your married friends outnumber your single ones or that you're not getting any younger. Your appointed time is linked directly to *your* purpose, not your homegirl's.

I'm trusting in God's timing because He created time, and because of who I know Him to be, and what He has already done in my life: the countless times His hand of protection has been on me (car accidents that I just barely avoided… life changes I wasn't yet ready for) and how He's aligned me with other unexpected blessings when I needed them (be it a career opportunity or even a credit on a bill). I also know what's happened—the unnecessary pain I've caused myself—when I've ignored His timing and tried to do things my own way.

I'm trusting in God's timing because I've rushed things before.

Be Careful What You Ask For

I met him shortly before Memorial Day, at a gas station, of all places. I was looking at his friend, but he was looking at me. It's funny how often it's happened that way for me. I liked his confidence and his smile, so I gave him my number. Before the end of the summer I knew I'd found something special.

Something different.

Maybe it was the way he could see through me and tell me about myself with love and love me anyway. He was even tempered, like my grandfather. No yelling. No name-calling. Unselfish. And he valued my counsel. It's easy to submit to someone who seeks your opinion and respects it. He didn't always take my advice, but I could count on him to mull it over and willingly acknowledge when I was right.

He commanded my respect by not demanding it. But, even still, I had concerns.

He hung around some young-acting people and ended up defending them in bar fights three times that summer—three times too many. And he drank like a man who had something he was trying to forget. But he was serious about us; of that I had no doubts. He introduced me to his family, took me to his church, and started talking marriage long before it ever entered my mind. Because of his insistence, I eventually dismissed my uncertainty and took his word that we were growing in the same direction.

After all, this was different. Right? Not for the reasons that I'd thought.

A few months before he and I met, my then-roommate had a guest over—a man who was not her then-boyfriend. I heard way more than anyone needed to, and her impassioned groans taunted me from down the hall as I tossed and turned in the night, trying to tune out long enough to fall asleep on the hard, unrelenting floor (I didn't have a bed back in those days.) Out of frustration and acute loneliness, tears streamed down my face, and I asked God why I was single when people in relationships were abusing the blessing. I'd worked hard to be open to commitment, to be able to let my guard down with a man. And isn't life supposed to be better—*easier*—when you give your life to Jesus? The things I was learning at church and hearing on Christian radio hadn't yet prepped me for this.

Overcome by emotion I pleaded with God to send me a mate, and I uttered aloud seven words no woman should ever say—they still ring in my ears.

"I don't care if he isn't ready."

If I'd had any idea what I was about to get myself into, I would've kept my mouth shut.

Accepting the Truth

Drama ensued in our relationship, and it extended years beyond our first—and final—breakup. Eventually, though, he did confess, "I'm not ready for all the things you are." Though he loved me enough to want to move forward, he recognized that his character wasn't able to sustain the vision he'd been selling both of us. I didn't understand that back then. I thought that if you want something and you're not ready then you just *get* ready. "What exactly is so hard about it?" I'd wondered. We all have a different call on our lives and learn and grow at different paces. And God works differently in each of us, and only to the degree that we let Him.

But the bombshell came when my ex added, "And you're not ready either."

Hold up.

Him not being ready I could see—but how was *I* not ready?

Among other attributes, I'm a good cook, I don't cheat, I'm intelligent, emotionally stable, I don't go around picking fights with my man (or anyone else, for that matter), and I learned long ago the power of a tamed tongue (though I wish that more men would leave the smart-mouthed comments in *their* heads).

My ex's words stayed with me for years after. Despite the questionable choices he made in his own life, there were quite a few times when God spoke wisdom to me through him. And eventually I saw that he was right. Even though I'd already learned some hard lessons and come out better for them, I needed to spend some additional time on a few others, including forgiveness (repeatedly, not just when it's convenient), perseverance, humility, faith, and timing.

And my lifestyle back then would not sustain the nurturing that a marriage needs, especially with someone who didn't have a similar purpose for his or her career. When you love your work, it's easy to substitute career highs for personal fulfillment, but what do you really want to achieve and why? Who are you doing it for? Most jobs aren't created with families in mind. You will have to make choices, and there are only 24 hours in a day.

I think our culture and values have made it more difficult for individuals to discern their appointed time for marriage and get into position for it—or to know if they're even called to marriage at all. There are too many distractions from the things that really matter; it's far more enjoyable to focus on ourselves. We expect that we'll get things our own way and live life on our own terms. It's easy to forget that our days are numbered.

But if you're not paying attention, your appointed time could pass you by.

—**Ericka Boston**

Ericka Boston is an accomplished journalist and is currently the senior editor at Sister 2 Sister *magazine.*

CHAPTER 11

Lessons from My Father

THE WESTERN WORLD HOLDS TIGHT TO THE BELIEF THAT you can't pick your family. What mystics believe, however, is far different. Ascended Masters teach that through free will, our family members decided together to make this journey on earth as part of a microcosmic family, sealing our DNA-embedded karmas together. That we would take the paths necessary, real or imagined, to help each other elevate our consciousness and release our souls from previous hurts or harmful pacts made in previous lifetimes.

I have not always seen eye to eye with my father, or understood where he was coming from. This, if I were to rely on mystic teaching, is more about me not always remembering why we chose to share a journey of growth than about our being different. Over time, the lessons he has imparted—both through his actions and, more profoundly, his inactions—have shaped my ability to see beyond my own hurt or confusion. I can examine my actions and the actions of others more emphatically, and understand why forgiveness is the most necessary action humans can take on the journey that is theirs.

Lesson #1: It's the Way You Say Things

My father, Noel Samuel Cole, was born the second-oldest son in a family of six in Kingston, Jamaica, in 1937. He never went to high school because he had to financially assist his mother, Edna, after his father, Oswald Cole, died of pneumonia. He remembers his father being extremely strict—ready to shout and spank first, and ask questions later. That wasn't the case with Daddy. Known more for sporadic ranting when he was peeved, he rarely gave spankings while I was growing up. But the boom in his voice when he wanted to emphasize the importance of something could reduce you to tears, and was more painful than the sting any strap could ever deliver.

I remember he and I taking the first car I had, a small two-door he purchased secondhand, out for a drive once. I began to pull away from the curb a little too fast and an oncoming car had to swerve to avoid us. I laughed nervously.

"This is serious, yuh nuh," he said, his Jamaican patois echoing off the car's interior. "Yuh tek dis for a joke?" as he kissed his teeth in that long drawn-out way only West Indians do.

"No, Daddy," I stammered, feeling utterly embarrassed as heat flushed my face. I drove home more carefully and slowly while listening to his long discourse of how driving is a serious "ting," what if I had gotten into an accident, I must be careful, all at a decibel level so high it was equivalent to a block party's speakers.

I was nineteen, but the tone in that verbal lashing reduced me to a five-year-old. The root of his speech wasn't about embarrassing me, however. At its core, it was about him being fearful that I would harm myself, or others, should I not be more careful. But who can truly hear that level of concern over his Jamaican din? That taught me one of my most valuable people lessons: It's not what you say but how you say it that matters. Words are the most powerful forms of expressions. Emotions of joy and pain manifest themselves with equal vigor. Both can penetrate and pierce the heart. And no matter what any nursery rhyme says, words do hurt.

It would take me a few years into adulthood to figure out the best way to express concern. I morphed from saying what was the problem too sternly, which left anger lingering in the hearts of others; to not saying anything, which didn't make the problem go away and left me still upset; to relying primarily on the art of diplomacy to obtain clarity. To my father's credit, time would show a different side of his transformation. One day, about 10 years later, when my brother, father, and I were together in our kitchen, the conversation turned to my driving. My brother, the speed demon with a lead foot, suggested that I drove too slowly. But my father, who had had more opportunities to observe my driving since that first incident, quickly countered in the same impassioned voice: "No, she's a good drivah."

Lesson #2: Silence Is Not Always Golden

As a young adult, I would hear my father bragging about my accomplishments to friends and family in Jamaica and to colleagues at his job. This always seemed odd to me and hard to accept because he never verbalized his pride while I was growing up or even as an adult. Phrases like *"I'm proud of you," "you did a good job,"* or other sorts of encouragement were not a part of his Caribbean DNA. His generation reasoned that you are expected to do well, so why should you receive accolades for doing, as Chris Rock says, what you are supposed to be doing? And while that concept is true in many areas, private and public acknowledgment is sometimes the very reason people do what they are supposed to.

I remember the working relationships I had with my second assistant and a steady pool of creative freelancers, including a fashion stylist and hair and makeup artists. I was a first-time manager. One day, after we'd worked together for about a year, the stylist casually remarked that I only said something when there was a problem, and that it was rare to hear me sing praises when I liked something. Later, when my second assistant made a similar comment, I had to stop and think.

I, like my father, was oblivious to the basic need of people to hear approval. I had grown up without it, measuring myself against a particularly sharp internal yardstick of what constituted a job well done. I didn't seek approval or validation from others for the work I did, and little did I know they were seeking it from me. What I communicated to the people I worked with—the people with whom I spent the majority of each waking day—was lacking the same level of Daddy-warmth as my childhood. They needed vocal validation.

My silence, for some, indicated that I did not value their contributions. They discounted my actions, as I had my father's. My father's nonverbal expressions, to me, didn't validate my importance to him. But this was the caveat I eventually learned: Just because pride and love isn't expressed in a manner you expect doesn't mean it doesn't exist.

The trick is in understanding each person's makeup. Some people are more comfortable expressing their feelings verbally and some, who aren't as comfortable with words, rely on actions to express how they feel. While my father didn't say "I love you," he showed how much he did in small ways: by making me breakfast every morning, by buying me a car after I learned how to drive (though that primarily was at my mother's urging), by bragging to his friends about me and my accomplishments, and by always giving an overly emotional card on my birthday and on Valentine's Day. In deciding who I wanted to be, I learned that silence isn't always golden. But it can speak volumes when you become still enough to hear.

Lesson #3: Hustle Is as Important as the Flow

When I was an undergrad, my father secured a part-time job for me as a telephone operator at the hospital where he worked, and I remained there after I graduated to supplement my meager assistant editor's salary. I worked every other weekend, from either 7 a.m. until 3 p.m., 11 a.m. until 7 p.m., or 4 p.m. until midnight. Sometimes, like in college, I would work the overnight shift. If I had a concert to cover, I would work an eight-hour shift on a Saturday and then head out at midnight to cover an event I had to write about Monday morning. I remember him showing a special pride in that, claiming that my work ethic came from him.

Truthfully, both my parents can claim that trait, but my father, who never called in sick to his blue-collar job and was never late to anything, is always first in line for that attribute. He would work 10- and sometimes 16-hour shifts at the hospital, and from time to time he'd "get his hustle on" exporting clothing to Jamaica, which became a small, flourishing retail business. He'd even drive a taxi or do odd jobs to make extra money. That taught me the importance of diversifying revenue streams.

We weren't poor by any stretch of the means, as my brother and I never wanted or lacked for anything. The extra money was his to spend as he pleased. And while my father didn't talk about why he did the things he did, his actions showed us that life as a sluggard was no life indeed. No matter what you did for a living, there must be pride in having a strong work ethic. This meant caring enough to be on time, doing what you've been hired to do well, and knowing that if you want anything in this life, you have to work hard for it.

But there was another, deeper lesson. The focus on the hustle allowed for little quality time with my brother and I or our four half-siblings. His down time was spent with his childhood friends doing what grown men do when they get together: take their mind off their troubles, feel no pressure, and regroup to go back out again into the real world. As a result, there was no real bonding experience that occurred between my father and his children during our tween or teenage years.

While all his work seemed to put him in the black, it left his relationships with his immediate family emotionally in the red. This taught us all the importance of having that balance. My brother once relayed something his daughter told him that made him stop in his tracks: "You're never here. And when you are here, you're always busy." And he remembered that's how he felt about our dad when we were growing up. He made a quick adjustment.

My other brother, the eldest boy, raised his daughters with Daddy Days as a constant feature so they would never experience that level of disconnect. When I realized that I was allowing the demands of my work schedule to put weeks, even months between times I saw my family and friends, I too made a conscious effort to change. Missing special time with them made me realize that maybe, just maybe, it's time to knock how I'm handling the hustle.

Lesson #4: Speak Up When You're Hurt

When rifts between his brothers left him feeling broken, my father didn't speak against my uncles, and we weren't forbidden to contact those family members. He, instead, suffered in silence and allowed the hurt to permeate deep within. Many people retreat when they have been hurt, finding themselves unable or afraid to speak about it. But not speaking up about what bothers you, I've learned, is a gateway to a lifetime of regrets. If not addressed, that initial hurt Never. Goes. Away. It weaves itself into the recesses of our DNA, only to be uncovered by a similar trigger, and only to be healed when we address its presence and talk it through.

In my relationships with two different West Indian men, I relearned this lesson more vividly. When they said or did things that triggered an emotional reaction, I learned to first ask them, "Can you clarify what you meant by that?" Or to say: "When you did this, this is how it made me feel." That would often lead to a discussion that clarified their position and allowed me to separate what they did from whatever pain I was feeling, and that nullified my perceived hurt. But to remove the hurt, I had to go back to where it originated. Not from an accusatory perspective, but one from understanding for more clarity.

Ironically, when I told my father that I was going to start asking him some questions about things that have been unresolved for me, it opened a window of dialogue between us that has allowed him to set some records straight. He shared the backstories behind decisions he made during the early years of his and my mother's marriage that caused irreparable damage; he divulged events where he felt his trust was betrayed by some of my siblings.

I learned about many things that had happened to him about which I had been unaware. I listened and marveled at how much he kept bottled up. His speaking up caused a slow release of pain, and showed me a side of my father I would have never known had I not asked for an explanation. Sometimes we are so put off by what we believe someone has done to us, so consumed by our own emotions, that we forget that they could be hurting as well. And the only way to break through that hurt and cut that karmic cord is to simply talk about it.

Lesson #5: Love Has Everything to Do With It

My mother was my father's first real love. I say that because years after they divorced, after he had a live-in girlfriend, he would still call on their wedding anniversary. They have been apart for 25 years now, and he still does it to this very day. He is five years her senior, and they married at the ages of 20 and 25. They separated and came back together, eventually divorcing 25 years later. It was a slightly painful period for my brothers and I, yet necessary for them both.

When I look back on their relationship, I never question his love for her, despite what was going on. While I never heard him say it,

I would see it in the way he would play with her and the effort he made in presenting gifts on birthdays and holidays: a box inside a box inside a box, or some other elaborate effort. But love and gifts are never all it takes to make a relationship work.

Antoine de Saint-Exupéry once wrote: "Life has taught us that love does not consist in gazing at each other, but in looking together in the same direction." The latter was difficult for my parents. As I watched them struggle to coexist and grow together—she was more progressive, with great long-term vision; he was content to remain within the confines of what he knew in the moment, and didn't think about planning for tomorrow or the next year—I learned that when love for each other isn't placed above all, pride really does go before the fall. Compromise, trust and understanding are what make all types of relationships—romantic or platonic—flourish.

To love is a choice that requires active participation from both parties. It is not an automatic guarantee the minute one says, "I do." It takes work that no one had prepared my twentysomething parents for. I went through my own relationship struggles, I identified the traits I didn't want in a mate first, but only developed what it is I did want, or (more importantly) what truly mattered, later on.

The funny thing is, while I sought verbal validation from my father, I looked for the exact opposite in the men I was dating, judging them more based on what they did rather than what they said. After one particularly hard two-year relationship ended, my boyfriend and I remained, like my mother and father, close friends. And he has, yes, sometimes, stuck closer than a brother would. Not in a romantic way, but in a way that says, "I care for you and your well-being." Though we didn't work out, I learned that love doesn't go away just because the relationship has ended. But if you allow it, the relationship can move beyond the hurt and settle in a place of true trust, understanding, and yes, real love.

Today, my father and I do not speak as often as I would like. But then, we never did. While we both can be loquacious when the mood strikes, we can both also be people of few words, needing our space to just "be." Many times we would drive for hours on end without much being said between us. The usual causes—teenage angst, a generational and a small cultural gap (he was a Jamaican raising his child in the United States)—contributed to the silence. He relies on my mother, who lives in another state, to share how I am presently doing.

Yet when I look back over the years, I realize his love for me came out in the most unexpected ways: having my mother dress me up when I was a toddler, so he could parade me around Kingston and show me to his friends; taking hundreds of photographs of me at the ages of four and five, when he picked up photography as a hobby; making me a fried-egg-and-plantain sandwich every morning for breakfast from junior high to high school; walking me to the bus stop in the morning whenever Daylight Saving Time hit and the sun had yet to rise; sending adoring birthday cards filled with emotional sentiments; never saying, "Why don't you go to a less expensive college or study something other than fashion illustration"; saving copies of the first magazines I edited; or quoting words from some of my editor's letters.

These were the tokens of his affections. They were the proof to him—and, he hoped, to me—that he cared. As a child, I took those tokens for granted. As a young adult, I looked back and yearned to understand why he didn't give more, why he wasn't more present. But as we both grow older, and the more I accept the fact that he did the best he could because of where he was and currently is as a person, we speak more openly. And as I grow as a person, this leads to understanding, which leads to forgiveness, which clears the path for seeing and loving him for who he and I truly are: my father, myself.

—**Marcia Cole**

Marcia Cole is a gifted content creator and editorial strategist with more than 20 years as a magazineelevate oia corporations including Fairchild Publications, Vanguarde Media, Latina Media Ventures, Time Inc., Essence, and AOL. Cole wants to express special thanks to Kenrya Rankin for pulling this story out of her.

CHAPTER 12

Seeing My Way through Single

RELATIONSHIPS CAN MEAN DIFFERENT THINGS TO DIFFERENT people; however, as you get older, you refine the idea of what a relationship really means—how you want to share your life, and with whom. As a gay black man, I remain a hopeful romantic, but finding a suitable partner has proved to be a continual challenge.

I have often been told that I am considered a good catch—tall, athletic, attractive, educated, well traveled, etc. If that is indeed the case, why, then, am I nearing the end of my 40s as a single man? I don't know how many times I have met guys or been on dates, only to be asked, "Why don't you have a boyfriend?" or told, "I can't believe you're single." Well, believe it.

I guess I'm a good catch on paper only, because I have only had one romantic relationship that I would consider long-term (two years). I have yet to actually live with a romantic partner (which was being discussed when the aforementioned relationship ended). I have often asked myself why that is. Trust issues? Just can't find Mr. Right? Maybe a little bit of both.

During my younger years, I was very career-oriented. Work was always very important to me. While working my way up the corporate ladder in the retail management, consulting, and entertainment fields, I definitely did my share of dating, but as a young man, having a boyfriend/lover/partner was never really a priority. I always felt that the situation would somehow work itself out.

But you eventually get to a point in life where the people around you—friends, relatives, co-workers, and associates, both straight and gay—start to find partners and pair off. I liken it to an odd game of musical chairs. The music stops, and some end up in pairs on cushy loveseats, and one person ends up on a single, hard-bottomed, wooden chair. Will that be me? Is this my destiny?

Although growing up in a black family in the heart of a large black community did little to prepare me for a loving, thriving gay relationship, I don't cast blame. My parents have been married for more than 50 years and are still together, so the model of a supportive, long-term relationship was there in my youth. My belief—that the foundation of any relationship lies in the ability of both partners to love, trust, and listen—remains steadfast and true. But that loving, long-term relationship I feel I deserve has somehow eluded me.

The fact that the black community at large does not readily accept homosexuality as easily as the white community is an issue. There have been reams of material written about gay issues in the black community, mostly regarding the lack of acknowledgment and support and the clashes with black institutions (specifically, black churches and historically black colleges and universities). Ongoing dialogue is needed here, and not just filtered through the big themes in our community, such as the issue of HIV and AIDS in our communities or the shame that forces many gays and lesbians of color underground, living their lives on the down low. These issues are certainly important ones, but at a very basic human level, everyone wants acceptance, support, and love. These are fundamental human rights.

I am reminded of a young man I knew once, a physician of Jamaican descent. He was a member of my social circle at the time, and we eventually went out on a few dates. I was interested in moving the relationship forward, but it became evident to me that he was still in the closet and not out to his family and friends. We discussed the situation a few times, his discomfort increasing each time it was brought up. Yes, I agreed, the medical field is conservative. Yes, I agreed again, it would be a difficult conversation to have with his religious Jamaican family. Yet, I encouraged him to do so. Unfortunately, he declined, giving in to his fear of how it would affect these relationships if his truth were revealed.

Needless to say, that relationship was short-lived.

I feel that when we are truly able to accept ourselves for who we are, then those around us, those who really love us and care about our well-being, will accept us as well. Now, there may be a journey for them to *get* to that acceptance, as was the case for my own parents, but to my way of thinking, that journey is well worth it. As a mentor told me long ago, if you love me, love me for who I *am*, and not who you *think* I am or who you *want* me to be.

I also remember ongoing conversations with many single straight black women, colleagues of mine during my long stint in the entertainment business. There was a constant level of frustration on their part, too, when it came to finding a long-term partner. There were vigorous discussions about the inability to find a straight black man who could (a) deal with the demands of a woman working in the entertainment industry (long hours, late nights, frequent travel); (b) handle the fact that a woman could have close professional relationships with several other men; (c) not be intimidated by the fact that, by virtue of working in entertainment, a woman may have access to parties, events, venues, etc., that he may not; and (d) realize that a woman who is successful in the industry is likely not to be controlled. Most of these sisters preferred dating outside of the industry to maintain some sense of privacy—a separation of church and state, if you will. I remember these conversations vividly. Looking back on them now, some of these sisters were able work it out and find a suitable partner; several others remain single to this day.

Now that gay marriage is a reality in New York State, will I ever make that trip down the aisle? While I am in love with the idea of finding someone I would *want* to marry, I don't want to put the proverbial cart before the horse. First, let me find someone who I care about enough to love, support, debate, disagree with, honor, and make myself emotionally available to before I start throwing around the *m* word. I really believe that someone exists.

Someone who can share my love of films. Someone to suggest amazing books I should read. Someone who appreciates pop culture references. Someone who will join me in discovering new music. Someone who will join my quest to learn more about art. Someone who will share my passion for travel and join me in exploring the world. A shoulder to cry on, and arms to hold me when I need them. And he will have that in me.

Is he the "Homie, Lover, Friend" R. Kelly talked about in his hit song? Maybe not, but that man is real and he is walking this earth, and we are destined to find each other. We have to, because I believe in fate and I believe in faith.

I claim optimism as one of my strongest traits; as such, I remain hopeful. While it may sound like a cliché, I believe that there is someone for everyone, and that we are not meant to live our lives on God's green earth alone. I believe there is a man out there who I can share my life with. Maybe I need by to open my eyes and ears a bit more—he might be closer than I could ever imagine.

—**Marlynn Snyder**

Marlynn Snyder is the founder and creative director of Black Tree Marketing, a multicultural marketing and communications consultancy, and has an extensive background in entertainment public relations. Snyder is also a contributing blogger and cultural critic for the Huffington Post. *His writing has appeared in* Billboard, Vibe, *the* San Francisco Chronicle, *and other publications.*

CHAPTER 13

What the Hell Do I Know about Love?

I 'M A THIRTYSOMETHING BLACK WOMAN WHO HAS NEVER BEEN married. I've never even cohabited with anyone before. It's not because I'm crazy—I'm not. I've never hid in bushes wearing footies and flicking a flashlight on outside of a lover's house. I have all of my teeth, a college degree, and I take pretty good care of my cat, Ms. Lucy. All things considered, I'm a decent catch. So it baffles menfolk—thankfully—when they discover that I've never been close to jumping the broom.

So what gives?

"You're picky."

I've heard that from more men than I care to admit. Granted, most of these would-be suitors say that after knowing me for an entire martini, and I usually shrug them off.

"If anything," I've heard myself say for years, "I've not been picky enough." But lately, I've been spending a lot of time lamenting my single state. Maybe I am too picky?

And if I am, I blame my mom and dad. And my grandparents. And my great-grandparents.

I was blessed. I saw firsthand how awesome Black Love is. And it's thrown a wrench in my love plan. I've had to ask myself if perhaps what my parents had is forcing this single woman to make the wrong moves. I asked my mother why she married my dad. She gave me the most unromantic answer ever: "I knew he'd be a good father."

Now what now?

She backed up to explain. On their first date, my dad—in a thick, Southern twang—told her, "I have the greatest dad on earth." He regaled her with stories of my grandfather, who was his Cub Scout leader, his best friend, and his confidant. He talked about the values that my grandparents instilled in my uncles and aunt, but it was the way he talked about his dad that captivated my mother.

Men had tried to impress her before. But never had a man talked lovingly about his dad the way my dad had. It stood out to her. And even as she told me the story of their first date, she recounted it as if it had just happened the day before.

My mom went on to tell me that when she and my father eloped to a courthouse in Ohio back in the 1970s, she wasn't in love with my father. Bomb dropped.

Her decision to enter holy matrimony was a conscientious one. She wanted her future children to say the same thing about their dad that the country bumpkin she went on a date with had said about his.

This didn't exactly sound like the storybook love I hope to find one day. In fact, my father's proposal was the most unromantic proposal I've ever heard in my life. My parents were both 24 years old. My dad, a small-town boy from Alabama, was in grad school in Detroit. My mother, a big city girl from the Motor City, was finishing up her undergraduate degree.

My father, tired of my mom dissing him date after date, decided to get serious. My dad was a frat boy—I grew up hearing that all great black men are Alphas—and that gave him a saucy side, I'm sure. He asked my mother if she'd accompany him on a trip to a football game in Ohio. She accepted, and he called back to tell her which hotel they'd be staying at.

She then declined. No way was she interested in taking an overnight trip with a would-be suitor. She established to my dad early on that she had a higher moral fiber than that. And if you knew my mom—she swears like a sailor, and long before she earned her PhD, she was the leader of a gang on Detroit's west side—she's no angel. But when it came to love and relationships, she was going to get every ounce of respect she demanded.

That sent a message to my dad, who quite frankly wasn't used to women responding to him like that. She was an anomaly. And he fell in love with that. So he straightened up. And he flew right.

Shortly after that phone conversation, my parents had an argument. And anyone who dares to go head-to-head with my mother in some type of verbal anything is going to lose. This was likely the one argument she walked away from speechless.

"Why don't we get married?" my dad asked her. She accepted.

They did, in fact, make that trip to Ohio. And almost 40 years later, my mother can't quite measure how much in love with my dad she is. Growing up, there was a time where my family moved every few years—some years, it'd be a great job offer for my dad, other years, for my mother—and I've watched them support one another and grow in their career and in their love. They're best friends— the kind who do everything together, travel together, have the same group of friends, and live a fabulous life together. Thankfully, my parents haven't needed to deal with the "in sickness and in health" part of their vows. But I know, without question, how that part of their story will play out.

Thinking of my parents makes me challenge myself. I think a lot of us single, educated, black women holding out for the real thing get too caught up in semantics. The right lighting, the right music, the right meeting place the right... everything—it throws us off. When we really examine these power couples we're so beholden to, the common denominator isn't any of the aesthetics that we think we need to have in order to have some sort of victorious healthy, black relationship.

Instead, it often times is a story like Carolyn and Bill Carter—a woman who knows what she wants and what she won't accept, and a man who steps up to the plate to make it happen.

And that's the way it should be.

—**Kelley L. Carter**

Kelley L. Carter is an Emmy-award-winning entertainment journalist.

CHAPTER 14

The Clock Is Still Ticking

I MUST ADMIT THAT FALLING IN LOVE AND GETTING MARRIED has not been one of my life's top goals or priorities. Let me be clear: I want to get married and enjoy the benefits that come with having a loving, productive, and permanent partner in my life. However, I have not been too keen on dealing with some of the bullshit that is necessary to reach that point.

In my life, I have been in three long-term relationships. By "long term," I mean relationships that have gone beyond the three- to five-year mark. After the five-year mark I have been done—finished and ready to move on. It's not that I have an aversion to long-term relationships; it's just that I haven't been able to tolerate my partner's flaws. Now to be sure, I know that I am nowhere near perfect. It's just that I don't expect other people to pick up the slack for me.

I am well acquainted with the sacrifice and dedication needed to sustain a relationship. My parents were married for 36 years in what could be best characterized as a topsy-turvy relationship that nevertheless stayed its course until my dad's death in 1999. But when it has come to my own life, I have been not been willing to follow their example. I knew from a very young age that I was not the kind of person who would be willing to give the appearance of being in a happy marriage just to appease my friends and neighbors. I knew that I wanted more for myself and for my partner.

I freely acknowledge my faults: I am egotistical, territorial, and even somewhat manipulative and controlling. However, what's equally true is that I am also exceedingly kind, generous, and honest. I try to own my shit and live my life on terms that keep my self-respect intact. Unfortunately, this attitude has not moved me beyond first base, in terms of finding someone with whom I can spend my life.

I used to think that my career as a busy and successful media professional would keep me shielded from facing the hard facts about my dilemma. But the brutal truth is that although I enjoy a healthy sex life, at 47 I am still no closer to meeting lasting love than when I was 27. So what do I do? I know that I don't want to go into my 50s and beyond single. Yet I also don't want to be in a permanent relationship unless it feels real right.

What's the answer?

Well, I've renewed my commitment to be the best person that I can be, by working to improve my heart, mind, and soul. I am keenly aware that the clock is still ticking, so I feel that there is still hope.

—Gil Robertson, IV

Gil Robertson is a journalist, author, and lecturer based in Atlanta, Georgia.

PART II
MARRIED

We Be

I be a jazz riff
Staccato offering
Daring and free   all over you   scatting   back beats
With scaled tongues   running things
Lifting you in soft soprano   a single stroke
A pantomime tune

You be a blues tone
The straight line of bold design   a dive and submerge.
A valley and height   you are pulse and prayer
Still on my lips   a mood I long to be in.

Our children, they be a praise-song
A field holler   outside anything we've known
A memory   a gift   a two-song melody
We were born to hear   rising vibrato

We be
A medley never ending
Colliding breath into flesh
Prelude to an ancient coda.

—Lita Hooper

Lita Hooper is a poet and playwright whose work has been published in anthologies and literary journals. She lives and works as an educator in Atlanta, Georgia. Visit Hooper's website at www. litahooper.com.

CHAPTER 1

The Big Picture

HAVING CONFIDENCE AND A WILLINGNESS TO WANT IT TO work—these are the factors that have kept my marriage successful. They, combined with our ultimate passion for each other, allow us to focus on the big picture in our lives and relationship. We both understand that we've made a commitment to see our relationship work because we sincerely want the best for each other.

As a man, you have to understand that women really, really need quality time, like having a conversation or going out together. We men like the quick solution, but often it's just about being present and listening.

For example, she might tell you, "The washing machine and the dryer have both gone out and the lights need to be changed." Okay, all right, I hear you, let's get it done. But she wants to talk about why it needs to get done and what time. She wants to talk about, "Well, the dryer door…" She wants to tell you every detail about what makes it broken. She wants you to hear it.

Sometimes it's not even about the washing machine and dryer. Sometimes it's about you, or the relationship, or something that's bothering her. That's her way of getting her mood together, to express that. So you have to know when it's just about the topic at hand, or when it's about something deeper than that. Some days I just want the quick answer. Then some days I'm like, "Okay, I know she needs to open up and vent, and get some things off her chest."

I've learned to listen carefully to my wife. This enables me to identify with her emotionally so that I am able to address her needs. Otherwise, I might pick the wrong battle or the wrong path and look insensitive. It's important to know that a woman needs a sensitive man more than she needs a macho one.

My wife and I are both spiritual, which is a quality that I believe a couple needs to have in common. Faith is one of the main things that keep us going, and our ability to move through our relationship together with love helps, along with forgiveness—more on her part than mine.

There's a temptation that comes with celebrity, and sometimes men in particular have that weakness. I'm not going to lie—it has been a weakness in my life more than once. But the key is to keep pressing on and to keep asking God for the strength. Because if you don't, all that looks good becomes available, or you become available to it.

Even though there's an age difference, my wife is just as mature as any other woman. My wife is a woman who can stand her own ground. That matters, because just knowing that people desire your man is a challenge. Until you master feeling secure—until it's been proven that, okay, he ain't going anywhere—it's a challenge.

It's not always easy to find the ideal partner, but I think getting rid of the idea of the "perfect mate" or the "soul mate" is the key. That keeps you blind to what's really *real* in a relationship.

It doesn't help to keep looking for that perfect relationship. Once you think you're in it, that perfect relationship becomes tested. Yes, you will have some days, months, and maybe even some years that are perfect. But if you're looking for it to be like that all the time, you're going to end up in divorce court. You're going to end up starting over again. You're going to end up unhappy, because nothing perfect really exists.

As time goes on, we all find things in the personalities of our partners that maybe were okay in the beginning, but later they aggravate you. However, it's important to look at the big picture of what you're trying to create together and determine if your partner's flaws are worth losing this person and starting over again in another relationship, only to find the same flaws. I now recognize that by embracing the big picture of my relationship, that I am committed to totally mastering the art of evolving as a man and investing in my wife's growth as well.

—Anthony Hamilton

Anthony Hamilton is a world-renowned platinum-selling R&B recording artist. Visit his website at www.anthonyhamilton.com.

CHAPTER 2

The Tooth Fairy, the Easter Bunny, and the "Perfect" Marriage

THERE IS NOTHING QUITE LIKE THE WIDE-EYED WONDERMENT of a child who believes in something with all her heart. That moment when what she imagines suddenly seems real can be nothing short of magical. I've had such moments in my life—many of them well beyond my childhood years. We all have.

When I first learned that there was a jolly fat man who delivered presents to all the children of the world once a year—free of charge—I was convinced that this was the best thing ever. Think about it: All I had to do was be reasonably good for a mere 364 days and on day 365, an old bearded man in a red suit would sweep down from the North Pole with a team of reindeer, shimmy down my chimney, and leave me every single toy my heart desired. He knew my name and my address, and he even knew if I had been bad or good. But here's the kicker: He did this for every single child in the entire world all in one night. What did my eight-year-old mind think of that? I thought it was amazing, of course.

It wasn't until I had a few more Christmases under my belt and caught my grandparents hiding gifts a couple of times that I finally grasped what I should have realized all along: that whole Santa thing—so not real. In fact, I concluded, it was impossible! Still, when I grew up, got married and had children of my own, I told them all about ol' St. Nick and, like me, they bought it hook, line, and sinker.

Believing in Santa was fun while it lasted but learning that he wasn't real—not so much. The same goes for the Tooth Fairy and the Easter Bunny. And yes, the same holds true for the perfect marriage.

Every young girl imagines herself floating down the aisle, gazing lovingly into the eyes of the perfect man. She dreams of having the perfect house, the perfect life, and the perfect marriage. But the minute she learns that her husband hates doing yard work, and he loathes shopping, and he despises her mother, it's like finding Mom and Dad hiding Christmas presents and devouring Santa's milk and cookies all over again. The myth is shattered and life as we know it is over.

Unfortunately, adults don't handle this epiphany as well as children. Kids move on and find other things to believe in. They don't try to make the Tooth Fairy real even though they know she's not. Adults, however, are a different breed. Once we find out that marriage is not the picture of perfection we hoped it would be, one of two things will happen: we try to mold our mates into who we would have them be; or we get on the next thing smokin' to divorce court, toss out the marriage like an old shoe, and start over again. If we're lucky, though, we'll discover what we should have known all along: There is no such thing as a perfect marriage.

Now, this might sound strange coming from someone who has been married for 25 years—to the same man, mind you—but it shouldn't.

My husband and I have been through many, many ups and downs. I've learned things about him that, had I seen them earlier, would have sent me running for the hills. He *might* say the same thing about me. Actually, I'm *sure* he'd say the same thing about me. Once the newness of a relationship wears off and you no longer have to pretend to be Mr. or Mrs. Perfect, you gradually fall back into being who you really are—and so does your mate.

Unfortunately, many marriages don't survive this period because, in many instances, people don't fall in love with real people. They fall in love with an ideal. They fall in love with the idea of marriage. They fall in love with the vision of who they think their spouse can and should be. They fall in love with a fantasy that dissipates quicker than you can say "ho, ho, ho." And no matter how many times they are disillusioned, they hold fast to the notion that perfection awaits them. In fact, they firmly believe themselves to be the perfect mates and they are convinced that they should settle for nothing less than perfection. They're wrong on all counts.

Being successful in marriage requires many things, including love, respect, selflessness, and honesty. One of the most essential, but often overlooked, ingredients is maturity. If you want to have a long-lasting relationship, you must simply grow up and realize that the notion of the perfect marriage is right up there with unicorns, Bigfoot, and yes, Santa Claus.

Now does that mean that you should settle for anything and anyone? Not at all. Abuse, whether it is physical or emotional; infidelity; incompatibility—these are all good reasons to end a marriage. Sometimes people simply don't fit. But the mature husband or wife knows the difference between a normal human being with a few annoying idiosyncrasies and a violent, demented philanderer who doesn't value you as a person or as a mate.

This also doesn't mean that you should stop working on your marriage. It's like the saying goes: "Shoot for the moon. Even if you miss, you'll land amongst the stars." Strive for perfection, if you must, but don't be discouraged and throw in the towel if you don't achieve it. Better yet, don't be disappointed when "perfection" looks like something other than what you imagined it to be. Perfection may not be tall, dark, and handsome. It might be short, chubby, and reliable.

That said, maybe the perfect marriage *does* exist. Maybe it's the marriage that has survived all the disappointment, disillusionment, expectations, pitfalls, trials, and turmoil that are inherent in every union. Maybe it's the marriage that acknowledges its imperfections but remains intact anyway. Maybe it's the marriage that does not rely on hype and fanfare for sustenance; the one that has matured to the point where both participants realize that imperfection is real, human, and normal. Maybe it's the marriage that has learned to be perfectly imperfect. But you'll never know if you don't stick around long enough to find out.

In the aftermath of believing in Santa, I was disappointed. I felt betrayed by my grandparents, by Santa, and by the entire population of the North Pole. *You can't trust anybody these days*, I thought. That lasted all of a day, and I was on to other things. I stopped believing in Santa Claus, but I didn't stop believing in what Santa represents.

He sets a standard for human kindness and he symbolizes everything that is good in the world. He reminds us that it is better to give than to receive. He teaches us that the fact that he isn't real doesn't mean we can't imagine he is. It doesn't mean we can't wish for everyone in the world to be more like him.

I guess the idea of the perfect marriage does that for us too. It gives us hope and a goal. It also makes us work harder, because as long as you believe, anything is possible. Right? True, but let's just remember to keep our expectations within reason and acknowledge the line between fantasy and reality.

After 25 years of marriage, I've discerned that there is a difference between trying to mold someone into the perfect mate and inspiring someone to be the best they can be. My husband and I still push one another to be healthier, stronger, and more creative, and we do that because it makes us better for *ourselves*—not just for each other. And even now, we still have the capacity to change. We still want to dig a little deeper, reach a little higher for ourselves —*and* for each other. We know when to push, how to push, and when to back off. We know one another's weaknesses and flaws. They're like those dingy old sweatpants that your husband refuses to throw out or that ugly vase that sits prominently on the mantel. They're a part of who we are as individuals and as a couple, and at some point, we have to accept that they just might be here to stay.

Still, I must admit that every now and then, I'm like that eight-year-old girl who wants to pretend that I didn't spy my grandmother hiding my Christmas presents, who swears up and down that I heard Santa's "ho, ho ho!" echoing from the rooftop and the cheerful jingling of sleigh bells in the distance. It's times like this that I'll ask my husband to do something that I haven't been able to get him to do in 25 years. I'll wait, gazing at him with wide-eyed wonderment, to see if this time, just maybe, he'll actually say yes.

—**Rhonda Freeman-Baraka**

Rhonda Freeman-Baraka is a screenwriter/producer based in Marietta, Georgia. Her most recent film, Trinity Goodheart, *premiered on the gmc network in August 2011 and was the network's highest-rated show in history. A noted journalist and media consultant, she made her entry into film in 2008, with the faith-based drama* Pastor Brown. *Through her company, ToKo Productions, Freeman-Baraka is currently developing the romantic comedy* Looking For Jimmy Lee *with real-life husband-and-wife team Boris Kodjoe* (Undercovers, Resident Evil, Surrogates) *and Nicole Ari Parker* (The Deep End, Soul Food, Welcome Home, Roscoe Jenkins). *Freeman-Baraka has also been commissioned to write a new gmc original movie slated for production this summer. Freeman-Baraka and her husband, Tony, are the parents of two children: Toni, 16, and Koran, 14.*

CHAPTER 3

—◆—

Black Boy Blues Suite: A Love Poem to My Father in E-Flat

"Love does not begin and end the way we seem to think it does. Love is a battle, love is a war; love is a growing up."

—James Baldwin

"Speaking indifferently to him,
who had driven out the cold
and polished my good shoes as well.
What did I know, what did I know
of love's austere and lonely offices?"

—Robert Hayden

LIKE MANY SOUTHERN FOLK, MY DAD FELT TRUTH WAS BEST served over a hot plate of comfort: fried chicken, mac n'cheese, collards, cornbread, and tea sweet enough to induce a diabetic coma. Laughing heartily from our portly post-thirtysomething bellies, we *always* departed our meals with a ritualistic embrace that expressed the way we love, as well as our raw emotions—bold, nonconforming, and insistent on having their way. Far removed from the icy winters of our discontent, we, quite purposely, had resigned from our once-lonely offices of Firm Father and Stubborn Son.

Men are never taught to love. We're never encouraged to sit in the "corner of ourselves" long enough to reason that self-loathing isn't the only option. Black Man Blues is a kind of blues solo often played to a rapt audience of one. I, like my father before me, piece-mealed my manhood in secret. Rather naïvely, in my mama's-boy youth I looked upon my father with contemptuous eyes, placing my teenage torments and the emotionless affair that had become my parents' marriage solely on his shoulders. I failed to notice the facts: my father was working a full-time job, squeezing in part-time hours at a package store, teaching me his patented jump shot for hours every weekend, attending nauseating PTA meetings, volunteering for the Empty Stocking Fund, coaching youth baseball leagues in a three-piece suit, and sponsoring my biweekly haircuts without fail.

I wanted perfection. He chose to be purposeful. I wanted the world. He furnished necessities. His calloused, slavery-stained hands, which could recount picking cotton in Georgia fields and cleaning rooms alongside his mother (who eked out a living as a hotel maid), told more stories than his closed mouth could ever muster.

I steeled myself in a defensive posture, turned my pain inward, and decided emotional unavailability would become the order of the day. We dueled like knights around an ignorant table, never once conceding that we were both responsible for turning up the uncomfortable silence that had sadly typified our rocky relationship. I was well into my undergraduate years before I realized I had never truly developed the capacity to love. How in a society where men are expected to cry in the dark—if they show any heart at all—would I develop the emotional maturity necessary to sustain a functional relationship with a life partner? When I moved cross-country in the pursuit of higher education, I carried both the fancy luggage set my beaming grandma and great aunt had purchased and also the burden of facing unchecked black male vulnerability for the very first time.

The United States' archaic visions of manhood have little room for elasticity. I, unwittingly, had begun to mimic my father's inability to express love in the raw. His flawed communication with my mother began to spill over into how I conducted my own relationships. The tragic victims were the women to whom I could never hand over my heart. I dated them all: models six feet tall with flawless etiquette, who could turn sidewalks into fashion runways; round-the-way girls hooking up chicken and red Kool-Aid while tidying up my abode; scholars who dabbled in quadratic equations for fun; activists who eschewed the sweetest liberation theologies; thespians who expounded on themes in the varied works of Nikki Giovanni and Amiri Baraka; and independent women fighting the powers that be with baby in tow. Despite the love that exuded from their beings, my daddy issues prevented us from reaching an accord. Some women were pushed away by my emotional ineptitude, some were frustrated by my bouts of chauvinism, and others were about as compatible with me as mismatched socks. The result was an emotional roller-coaster that only squeaky-wooden-floor preaching, trips to therapy, and getting out of my own way could undo.

Through counseling and the unrelenting prodding of my grandma, whose stinging critiques of my foolhardy ways and "respect your father" refrains often rang in my subconscious, feasting on humble pie became an inevitable part of my maturation. It began with a gut-wrenching apology as I confessed treasonous acts like a tortured sinner at his first Sunday altar call. My father set aside his pride and accepted it. In choosing to embrace our own vulnerability, we delivered ourselves from generations of manhood miseducation. I began to see my father not as Superman, but as a human being with more in common with me than I could have ever imagined.

There is nothing sweeter than being released from a burden. Whether I realized it or not, love could not live in the presence of hate.

The greatest benefactor of the love that now anchors the bond of father and son has surely been my beautiful wife. Instead of inheriting damaged goods, as is the case in many dysfunctional relationships, she found in me an emotionally available partner who, by trial and error, developed the capacity to love uninhibited. Learning to love my father had made me more patient, kind, grounded, and understanding. By remixing my father's early vision of manhood, which emphasized the politics of providing over trying a little tenderness, I became a man well equipped with the coping strategies necessary to weather the joy and pain of a loving relationship.

Through our healing suite, my father and I rebuilt what I, in the arrogance of my youth, had steadfastly tried to tear down. We began to organically pepper conversations with, "I love you." Fist pounds evolved into unabashed hugs. Love became our rule with no exceptions. We became better men. I found my future. More than a decade would pass. Busy Bee became *our* spot.

Death, however rendered, is ripe with inconvenience. Nothing on God's red, black, and green earth prepares you to cope with finding your father's lifeless body in your childhood home. Not when his wise counsel had become as necessary as air. Not when after years of being a work in progress, our relationship was a fruitful and productive father-and-son relationship. Days after my father's passing, I attempted to pick up the pieces of my heart as I rummaged through a home once filled with spirited debates, the musical joy of the Stylistics, and talk of the grandson attending college at "The 'House." When I stumbled over a pair of worn basketball kicks I had loaned him ages ago, I pondered if I would ever be able to fill his shoes. By forgiving my transgressions, he had already proven he was man enough to walk in mine.

—Edward Garnes, Jr.

Atlanta native Edward M. Garnes, Jr. is an award-winning writer, educator, and counselor. He holds a BA in English writing from DePauw University and an MA in counseling from Michigan State University. His nationally acclaimed manhood tour, Sweet Tea Ethics, has featured brothers Dr. Cornel West and Clifton West. Garnes is also the founder of fromafrostoshelltoes.com.

CHAPTER 4

---•---

Strong Women and Gentle Men: The New Compatibility

You know her. She's that passionate, self-assured woman whose opinions are easily and often expressed. She knows what she wants, and how to get it. She's got no time for foolishness; she's about living the good life. She's a fervent force of nature to be reckoned with. She's your sister, your BFF, your instructor, your boss. She's YOU!

She's a strong woman who's found compatibility in her love life. She's the prize of a mate so sure of his strength that he can gently bring out the best in the woman he's learned to love. Their happiness is the basis for this essay. This is a tribute to couples everywhere who have found harmony in discord and music in mayhem.

I
F THERE IS ONE WOMAN WHO EXEMPLIFIES MY NOTION OF THE fervent, impassioned, self-assured, accomplished woman in a strong-gentle coupling, it's Michelle Obama. Her profile, based on the stories we hear and read about from her husband, mother, and brother, give us insight into this extraordinary woman's marriage. She is the First Lady to the leader of the free world, and his respect for her is gently yet powerfully expressed. His pride in her efforts to bring attention to issues facing our troops and their families, her concern for the less fortunate, and her role modeling for American motherhood is obvious in his public comments and loving glances. And yet, our president is a decisive, action-oriented leader, held in high regard around the world. President Obama combines the tenderness of fatherhood with the boldness of international leadership flawlessly.

Mrs. Obama was already a successful attorney before her marriage. As the story goes, Barack Obama once worked for her. She's a no-nonsense woman who speaks her mind and—according to her brother—would have been unhappy about a favorite aunt's possibly less-than-favorable impression of a would-be politician like the little-known Barack Obama before they wed. She's become an attentive, disciplined mother who plants vegetables in the White House garden and whose children set their own alarm clocks for school each day. And there's that easy, welcoming smile! This elegant, stylish, loving woman is an exquisite example of a strong, successful woman respected by the man who loves her.

Marilyn and Kevin, our second couple, represent marriage in the new millennium. They dated and lived together for three years before getting married. Now in their early thirties, they are the proud parents of a daughter named Sasha, soon to be a year old.

A strikingly beautiful woman, Marilyn's first love was theater and dance, which is evident in the graceful way she moves. Marilyn is also a compassionate person. Her quiet strength is evident almost immediately when you meet her. She's the type of person who can handle almost anything with courage and grace. That's why her profession as a drug counselor suits her. It also pays the bills.

Kevin, on the other hand, is the talker, the dreamer, the builder. Equally pleasing to the eye, you can see that he and Marilyn belong together. Nonetheless, they are polar opposites. Kevin is volatile. If a job he's doing isn't going according to specification, he's likely to junk the project and begin again. He's a perfectionist, but perfection can come at a high price to a person who is trying to build a business.

Marilyn is the practical one in their relationship. Though she loves theater and dance and is involved with community theater, where she finds personal expression and fulfillment, she's mindful of her day job and its value. Kevin, on the other hand, is stubborn once he gets a thought in his head. Any change in thought must come from him, because he doesn't take advice easily. To him, suggestions are criticisms in disguise, and they often result in hurt feelings. He's an entrepreneur and a maverick of sorts. He creates brilliant home and industrial security systems that protect with the convenience of a phone call. He can write sophisticated computer code like a good teacher writes lesson plans.

The key to the success of their marriage is in balancing Kevin's need to be an independent business owner with the reality of supporting a wife and daughter. What makes this possible is how Kevin and Marilyn relate to one another. Although he's in technology, he is essentially a creative type and, as someone who loves the arts, Marilyn understands and supports his passion. She showed her support by taking on the responsibility for the increased expenses a child demands and held on to her position at a social work agency. Sure, she'd like to devote more time to community theater, but she's pragmatic and believes in her husband's dream, no matter how choppy the waters are. That's when Marilyn's quiet, calming manner helps soothe Kevin's frustrations, just as it seems they're going to overtake him. Marilyn expects his behavior to need her steady hand, and she's there to extend it at will.

I asked Marilyn how she managed to keep the peace at home. She explained that her mother was her role model. Her mother had lived the example Marilyn has since emulated in her own marriage. Marilyn has been able to shoulder their mutual plans to purchase a home, create the security business, and start a family, even when Kevin seemed most scattered. He sees Marilyn as his wife, his muse, and the reason he's happy to come home at night. She's loving, encouraging, forgiving and, most of all, she believes in him. They listen to each other and care for each other's needs.

Marilyn and Kevin operate their relationship like a business. Each knows the other's assets and liabilities, and each is willing to overlook that which is difficult to make room for the achievable. They focus on what's workable, and regard the rest as noise. It's not easy, but few things are more rewarding when two people are so different. Strong women are not always outspoken, fervent, or impassioned. They can be steadfast like Marilyn when dealing with a creative, driven mate whom they love. They make it their business to understand and make coming home bliss. Their paradise is big enough for all their dreams.

Donna and Burt were college sweethearts who married after dating for seven years. Although they were both just 28 years old at the time and thus still pretty young, Donna was glad to get the ring on her finger. She'd been a bridesmaid in four of her friends' weddings in the previous three years and was thrilled to avoid the always-a-bridesmaid-never-a-bride trap.

After honeymooning in a tropical locale, Donna and Burt settled into an apartment just three blocks from his parents' home. At the time, Donna wasn't the least bit bothered by the proximity of her in-laws. It was a lovely neighborhood, and the price was right for a couple just starting out.

With two busy careers in the financial sector, it wasn't unusual for either of them to work ten-hour days. Nevertheless, Donna made an effort to get home as early as possible so she could cook and share a meal with her husband. There was only one problem: Burt was in the habit of stopping by his parents' house. There, he'd usually eat dinner, so he wasn't hungry when he got home.

At first, Donna let it go. She chalked it up to missing his mom's cooking. She was sure it would pass and he'd come home to eat with her. He didn't. Soon she found herself spending every Sunday at his parents' place for dinner. No matter how many hints she threw him, Burt just didn't get it. He'd lived with his parents up until three months before he and Donna got married. And even then, he was eating at his parents' home at least four times a week. Donna, on the other hand, had lived on her own for three years. Sure, she'd have dinner at her parents' house on occasion, but it wasn't a regular habit.

As Donna explained it, the upside of working on the trading floor on Wall Street was that she wasn't afraid to speak up. She let Burt know that she didn't appreciate working all day, getting on the train, and rushing to get home to make him dinner—only to have him eat with his parents. They were a family now. Burt apologized, and it seemed like they were getting on track until she found herself having dinner with the in-laws every Sunday.

Then one Saturday Donna received a visit from her mother in-law, who was bearing a bag of goodies. She'd come to teach her how to make her son's favorites just the way he liked them. By the time her mother-in-law left, Donna was fuming, but she took the lesson with more than a few grains of salt.

To get some perspective, Donna called her mother for some advice on how to handle the situation. Her mother advised her to calm down and look at the situation rationally. Had his mother really done something bad? All she did was show Donna how to make Burt's favorite foods, and since she now had that knowledge, wouldn't that make him more likely to eat at home with her? Donna's mother had been married for 30-plus years and had gone through the same situation with her own mother-in-law. Still, she encouraged her to talk to Burt about her feelings so everything was in the open.

Her mother's advice was right on the money. Once Donna calmly explained how she felt to Burt, he understood her position. Soon, he was home for dinner every night, as Donna had more than mastered his favorite foods. From the outside looking in, the couple's problem seemed small, but had they let it fester, it would have grown and ultimately driven a wedge between them.

———

Problems, both large and small, can become like an 800-pound gorilla in the room. Defining the 800-pound gorilla in every marriage varies from couple to couple, as does how they deal or don't deal with it. What works for Marilyn and Kevin, or Donna and Burt, may not work for other couples with different issues. Some 800-pound gorillas are problems about money, career, child rearing, ex-spouses, former boyfriends or girlfriends, sex, and, now, with the advances of modern technology, we can add BlackBerrys, iPhones, and the Internet. Now that technology is accessible 24 hours a day, 7 days a week, it's easy to ignore the gorilla. Thus, the underlying issues are never addressed until the gorilla doubles in size. By that time, most couples can't ignore it anymore, but don't know how to deal with it.

The key here again is communication and making an effort to tune out the discord and just talk. Professional help is always available. Ultimately, it's about love. As 1 Corinthians 13:4-7 states:

"Love is patient and kind; love does not envy or boast; it is not arrogant or rude. It does not insist on its own way; it is not irritable or resentful; it does not rejoice at wrongdoing, but rejoices with the truth. Love bears all things, believes all things, hopes all things, and endures all things."

It's the best way the strong women I know keep the 800-pound gorilla at bay!

—**M. Cecile Forté, PhD**

This essay is excerpted from Forté's book *Strong Women and the Men Who Love Them.*

Cecile Forté, PhD, has a national reputation as an author and a specialist in developmental education. She is a former academic dean at Suffolk Community College and also served as interim associate director for the Commission on Higher Education, a unit of the Middle States Association of Colleges and Schools. Forté is the author of three textbooks and two trade books, including the very popular Wise Women Don't Have Hot Flashes, They Have Power Surges!

CHAPTER 5

———•———

A Partnership on Every Level

I HAVE NEVER BEEN A BELIEVER IN THE KIND OF LOVE THAT YOU have to work at to achieve. In my opinion, love is something that happens naturally. That's the kind of love I've known with my husband, Gregory.

It was love at first sight. He called me immediately after our first date, so I knew he was infatuated, even though I wasn't looking especially cute on that occasion. It was during summer school and thus was really hot. I needed a perm in the worst way; my hair was standing all over my head like a hot mess. There must have been some sort of divine intervention that night, because from the very start it felt right—we were connected. You have to be open when the right person comes around, and that was the case for us.

Gregory and I were both fortunate in that we had good role models who shaped our view of the opposite sex. In my case, both of my grandfathers provided me with great examples of what I should look for in a man. My father's father was the first African American medical doctor in Shreveport, Louisiana, and my mother's dad was a businessman who owned a 500-acre farm in Grenada, Mississippi. Along with my mother, they instilled in me a sense of values about what partnership means between a husband and wife. In many ways, my parents were complete opposites, but their marriage stood the test of time. The same is true for Gregory and me; we have a lot of differences, but like my parents, our marriage has lasted because we share the same core values.

There was never a time in my life when I didn't want to pursue partnership on every level with the man I married. However, I also believe that the basis for any healthy relationship is for both parties to feel good about who they are, and recognize that they are individuals first and a married couple second. Even though you are a unit in marriage, it is still important that you maintain your individual identities. It is especially important for women to know that having someone take care of you is not an answer for not having your own identity.

I never wanted to be a person who was taken care of, and it's been my experience that most men who are serious about their relationships are looking for a woman with whom they can share a full partnership. A lot of women think that men want a Southern belle, or a clinging-vine type of woman, but I think the opposite is true. It's particularly the case today, as men have learned that they will need a strong woman who can help them build their lives and reach for their dreams. Successful marriages are built by people who have a genuine respect for each other and who contribute equally to their marriage and family.

For my children and all of the young people I mentor, I hope that my 43-year marriage sets an example that will guide them as they pursue relationships of their own. Today it is a lot more challenging for them to find a genuinely good person to partner with. I tell them that they can find love and build a good life with someone who shares their goals and aspirations. Despite the many outside forces that can influence couples to go in opposite directions, I want them to find partners with whom they can achieve a quality life filled with happiness.

The most important relationship in my life has been the love that I share with my husband. I know that I have been blessed to not only know romantic love with Gregory, but to also create a successful professional partnership with him in the business enterprises we have built together. For us, having romantic and professional success together has been the best of both worlds; but it couldn't have happened without trust, mutual respect, and most of all, genuine love.

—**Juanita Baranco**

Juanita Baranco is the executive vice president and chief operating officer of Baranco Automotive Group, which she cofounded with her husband, Gregory Baranco, in 1978. Baranco is a former assistant attorney general for the state of Georgia, and the first African-American woman to chair the state's Board of Regents.

CHAPTER 6

Love at the Corner of Putnam and Webster

ROWING UP IN THE 1970S ON PUTNAM AVENUE IN THE EAST End neighborhood of Plainfield, New Jersey, offered myriad diverse experiences. Such things as climbing trees, watching the seasons change, navigating friendships, and the importance of neighbors and neighborhood are on my near-endless list of what helped shape me as a person.

Noticeably absent were examples that spoke to matters of the heart, and I don't mean love and affection of family or friends; to be sure, those were in great abundance. I mean romantic love, husband/wife love, the kind of love they write songs about. In fact, as much as I hate to admit this, many of my early examples of romantic love came by way of television—sitcoms in particular. Such shows as *Bewitched*; *Lost in Space*; *The Brady Bunch*; *Love, American Style*, and others, always featured loving, if sometimes complicated, marriages. And no matter how the episodes unfolded, they'd invariably end with the husband and wife kissing and hugging their way to some new understanding, or at least with a tidy ending to whatever crisis defined that episode.

I must admit—and I mean this without any judgment—there was not much romantic love on display in my immediate family or in my local circles. My parents, Bill and Elizabeth Cathcart, loved my sister and I completely, of that there is no question. I truly believe they loved each other too, just not outwardly, or at least publicly. I don't have too many memories of them walking hand in hand or canoodling on the couch or giving each other warm farewell/hello kisses. Now, my mom passed when I was only eight years old, so I'm sure having such a short time to observe them had some impact.

After that, Dad kept his subsequent lady friends at a respectful distance, so I may be a victim of circumstance as much as anything.

However, even beyond my parents, I didn't really see public displays of affection from extended family or other couples in the neighborhood. I knew people who were married; lived together; and had kids, dogs, cars, and houses, but interpersonal interaction was not a neighborhood staple. Interestingly, I only remember one couple who held hands as they walked together: Vance and Nanci, the first interracial couple I saw in real life. Vance, who lived up the street on Webster Place, was a distant cousin of mine and an overall nice cat who was quick with a kind word and always seemed above the standard knucklehead activity that some of the other neighborhood guys considered normal. Nanci reminded me of Peggy Lipton, the actress from the early '70s television show *Mod Squad* who went on the marry music impresario Quincy Jones.

I distinctly remember seeing them walking down the middle of the street—*the middle of the street*—hand in hand and, I suppose, heart in heart. I also remember the derisive comments from many of the older black women in the neighborhood, including the ones in my family. "Look at that boy with that white girl, *hummmmph.*" If I had a dollar for every time I heard that refrain!

Their loving relationship made for great gossip, but few teachable moments. The neighborhood's reaction made me think Vance and Nanci were doing something wrong, that they were acting out of line. Looking back now, I realize that was a foolish attitude to have, but it reflected the times. I'm confident that viewpoint was not particular to my neighborhood or family. For the record, Vance and Nanci went on to marry, have children and, by most accounts, create a wonderful life together. Vance still chuckles when I tell him this story.

As I got older, the predominate images and examples of expressed love between a man and a woman still came via popular culture, specifically so-called Blaxploitation films—think *Shaft, The Mack, Superfly,* and countless others. Since I learned about sex on the street (no "sit down, son, let's talk about the birds and bees" convo for me), these films provided graphic examples of lovemaking, if nothing else.

Hell, my friends and I would often rate them by the number of sex scenes in them, well ahead of the action and violence (example: "Man, you get to see Pam Grier's titties!").

The brothers in these films were bad dudes, and by bad I mean *good*. They kicked ass, sexed numerous honeys, and drove cool, long cars. And, in absence of better, real-life examples, they provided guidance for me.

This so-called cultivation influenced not only my ideas about love, but also my views about black manhood and sexuality. It is near impossible to separate a man's approach to romantic love from his ideas about his own sexual self-awareness. How does romantic love fit into this concept? How can you be a strong black man and successfully incorporate the inherent vulnerabilities that come with letting go and letting love evolve? If you have an answer, I'm listening.

These contradictions have been a part of my life through every significant era. By the time I got to college, my beloved Howard University in the early '80s, the die was cast. Of course there were a few examples of outwardly loving couples on campus, but they didn't carry the day. If I ever heard a brother say he loved his woman, it was while we were alone, and in almost whispered tones. Sadly, I still remember how painfully awkward I felt when a woman told me she loved me. In fact, I think I said "thanks" the first few times someone said that to me. I guess that was better than saying nothing.

Needless to say, holding hands and open displays of affection were not a part of my DNA. I recall one college girlfriend screaming for me to grab her hand while walking down a city street in Washington, DC. I wouldn't comply. And after my college years, adult single life offered more of the same. I had lots of dates, plenty of sex, and a weird, distant relationship with love.

Somehow, I guess I came to view romantic love as a destination you strive for but never truly arrive at, like peace and happiness. Or, if you do get there, it's a fleeting feeling, akin to a warm breeze that engulfs you momentarily, then moves on and away.

Many years and many women have passed since my early days growing up on the corner of Putnam and Webster. I'm married now, yet still navigating the nexus of sex, love, and understanding.

My wife works with me. She's patient with me, and she tries to cope. I still hate holding hands, or hugging without a good reason. Non-sexual intimacy remains a major hurdle and, at this age, it may be a hurdle I never overcome. But as the experts say, the first step toward recovery is admitting there's a problem.

The odds of me changing are slim, but I know I need to try, and that has to mean something. I wish I could go back in time, run up the street, and grab hands with Vance and Nanci. I'm sure we would have made a lovely trio, and perhaps I'd be a better man.

—Christopher D. Cathcart

Christopher Darren Cathcart is a published author; a public relations, marketing, and brand development expert; a noted public speaker; and a social entrepreneur. In 1995, Cathcart founded OneDiaspora Group, a Los Angeles- and Washington, DC-based communications consulting firm. His first book, The Lost Art of Giving Back, *a how-to guide to volunteerism, was published in 2007. A graduate of Howard University, Cathcart is also a tireless community advocate, promoting HIV/AIDS awareness, working with at-risk youth, and supporting historically black colleges and universities, among other worthy causes.*

CHAPTER 7

————•————

My Great Love

PEOPLE OFTEN GASP WHEN I TELL THEM MY HOW LONG MY partner and I have been together. As if they've never heard of marriages and partnerships that have lasted and conquered the test of time. Yes, 13 years is a long time, but it's nothing compared to people I have known who have been together 40, 50 years. Admittedly, it's rare nowadays, especially in the African-American community, but it's not unheard of.

There is no secret or recipe to making a relationship or marriage last.

Although we are not legally married in the eyes of the law, what matters is the ceremony we had in Cancún, Mexico. There, in front of our friends, we committed to each other for as long as we are alive.

I knew I loved her from the start. How we met can be best described as right out of a movie scene—that's how it went down. We became friends at first, but a torrent of stomach-turning phone calls that left me lightheaded ensued. I grew brave and bold and told my mother I was in love—and with a woman. I didn't need intimacy to solidify that feeling, but it did. Then, for the first time after coming out to my parents, I understood what it was like to get unconditional love.

My coming-out process was very difficult, and it is still difficult being gay, considering I was brought up an extremely culturally homophobic environment. But I always knew love was love, period, and nothing was going to stop me from pursuing a relationship I knew I deserved.

Very few people get the opportunity to encounter their great love, and even fewer people get a chance at it more than once in their lifetime. I am one of those very fortunate individuals. I'm not saying being in a relationship is easy—it's work. I have learned over the years to appreciate my life partner. When we argue we don't always communicate right away, but when we are happy we share each other's joy. She's an introvert, and if you know anything about introverts, they like being by themselves often (if not all the time). I'm an extrovert. I live and feed off the energy of others, and therefore want to be around people all the time. And being polar opposites doesn't take away from the fact that we fight, we love, we cry, we make up just like anyone else—but more importantly, we accept each other as we truly are, holding ourselves in beauty and light despite it all.

I have invested time and love in this relationship, and after 13 years, we still have respect for each other, attraction, and love. But we're also still discovering things about each other and learning new things, and in the end it's about awakening to your own nature and experiencing the joys of others.

—Nava Yeshoalul

Nava Yeshoalul was born and raised in Ethiopia before she came to the United States at the tender age of 12. She considers herself a free-spirited writer and began experimenting with spoken word in college. She enjoys writing about her life experiences and coming-out process through her blog and poetry. Besides writing, Yeshoalul enjoys experimenting with various forms of art. She is a massage therapist, she fiddles with hammers and screwdrivers once a while, and generally likes to have her hands occupied. She lives in California with her wife of 13 years.

CHAPTER 8

Black Humanity and the Crisis of Home

I T IS NO WONDER THAT THERE ARE PROBLEMS IN THE BLACK community, captured in statistics and spirit and memory. How could things be otherwise? Black humanity is simply, in the final analysis, humanity. And human beings need their homes—not mere dwellings, not mere abodes—if they are to flourish.

Though marriage is a universal construct, there are all sorts of contexts for it. Some cultures use marriage to relegate women to what is considered a "naturally" subservient position. Some cultures, such as this one, lionize marriage in one breath and, in the next, lionize a commercialist and consumerist system that serves to undermine marriage.

Some cultures only allow people to marry if they are from the same privileged class or caste (they go on to discover the unique set of problems that privilege can bring). Others struggle to make ends meet; this brings another set of problems. Gays struggle for the recognition of their unions as marriages, and must suffer through a battery of doubts from their straight compatriots served up in pregnant pauses, jaded glances, and sly quips.

And if you are black in the United States and you marry, there remain long tentacles that still find their way from the bowels of history and into the lives of blacks as individuals and as a collective. There are specters that still haunt, and demons that still plague. And so it goes.

The notion of marriage, for anyone, is well known. It is a union, a commitment for the long haul—if not for life, then at least for as long as the children need to be raised, or for some other long period of time, toward whatever horizon does justice to the covenant made. It is not a commitment to be taken lightly. It involves shared space and the promise of mutual support concerning the exigencies of life; otherwise, it is not marriage, but something else. Some prefer to say that it is a union in the eyes of God. Yet, that is not all. For the *context* matters, and "the eyes of God" is not a context that we mere mortals can get our heads around, even if, for many, God holds an important place. It is the context that conditions our ability to enter into and negotiate a marriage, just as contexts condition our ability to enter into a business deal, a friendship, or a career.

To talk about black marriage is to talk about marriages within a nexus of contexts. In the black community, it is little wonder that the statistics concerning marriage seem so bleak. As blacks are human beings, how could it have been otherwise? The frustrated rhetorical question "Why can't we fix our problems?" is cogent, apt, and has its place. But we must be careful to avoid taking action. We can indulge ourselves in them, shake our heads, and point to the troubling statistics. But we must also, even as we point to the problems and possible solutions, remember *why*. Remembering why is important; it blunts the harsher criticisms and self-criticisms that can and do lead to despair. We don't want to indulge failure, but we must let love and understanding have a place in our analyses and rhetoric.

I read somewhere that in the early 1960s, it was believed that close to 70 percent of black households were headed by married couples. By 2002, this same source reported, that percentage had declined to around 48 percent, and close to 31 percent of black women were married. I often hear statements such as "Black women remain the most likely women to head single-parent households," and "Households headed by females are the most likely to be below the federal poverty line." And so on.

Understanding all of these data means understanding a great deal of cultural, economic, and racial crosscurrents, and I am not so sure that many of us do. These statistics are not what they are simply because of racism or feminism or consumerism or individualism, but because of all of these factors, and more that go unnamed. Many black women are wary of marriage for a variety of reasons that make their wariness quite rational indeed. Many reckon that, given the stress placed on black men by a range of factors, the likelihood of a successful marriage, or even of a nurturing long-term relationship, at least *seems* doubtful.

Statistics show that black men are much less likely to graduate from college than black women or white men, and the unemployment rate for black men still soars above that of white men. Unemployment among blacks has recently approached something like 17 percent. Even the black men who have overcome these factors and achieved relative economic and/or social success seem more focused on maintaining that success than establishing households with a spouse or partner. All of this creates headwinds for black relationships.

Anomie among the black poor is deemed the culprit in simplistic analyses of why black marriage seems to be waning, though it doesn't explain everything. The headwinds that affect black marriage do not only blow from *within* the black community. In the United States, a strong consumerist culture and rampant self-centeredness also lend themselves to the deterioration of black marriage, just as they lend themselves to the deterioration of family life (and financial prudence) more generally. Blacks, already weakened, are more susceptible to these forces than whites and other demographics, and have been, with certain exceptions, for a very long time. Blacks spend far too much and save far too little. We are drawn into the consumerism that exists in the United States, though we can afford it the least. We continue to be taken in by the constant siren song to buy more and more gadgets, clothes, and image-related items, instead of shares of stock or certificates of deposit. This renders many unprepared for the financial obligations that come with marriage, and financial stress is a leading cause of marital distress and marital failure, as we all know.

Of course, while it is true that anomic behaviors don't explain everything, they do explain *some* things. Another factor is that black boys and girls lack patterns they can follow that might guide them in such matters as choosing mates, setting up a household, creating a real home ("household" is a sterile sociological term; "home" speaks to the creation of a filial spirit), and providing the spousal and parental support needed over the long haul to make the home successful.

Many black girls have seen so few examples of successful men in their families that they harbor serious doubts about black men in general. Black boys, raised in so many households without fathers, lack exposure to the subtle-yet-crucial patterns of behavior and thinking needed to serve as good fathers and nurturers themselves (and this is not to say that only "maleness" can shape character, but it has an important place in homes with boys). Many, quite *rationally*, find support in gangs or among peers outside of gangs, and look to images in the media to serve as exemplars and role models. But such images can only show what is *possible*, not the processes required to achieve goals that, over a lifetime, establish success. Seeing the space shuttle take off is one thing. Building it is another. It is the long slog that creates success, not the enticement of glossy magazine images of black males in business suits holding snifters of brandy, or in military flight suits on the decks of aircraft carriers, though these have their place.

The confluence of these and other factors has led some to the curious conclusion that "marriage is for white people." Peeling back the layers of this seemingly insane conclusion, I interpret this to mean that only whites (so it is perceived), can afford to establish the foundations for a successful, long-term, and reasonably happy marriage—in *this* society—and therefore actually pull it off.

But while this conclusion may be curious, even troubling, it is not nonsensical. In fact, it is a reasonable conclusion, given the evidence. The belief that marriage is for white people can be better understood once you consider the factors arrayed against blacks, from the deliberately destructive to the merely insidious, corrosive, or vestigial (or all of these). The institution of marriage must be ceded to "other demographics" that have the wherewithal—financial, cultural, communal, and spiritual—to make it work.

It is often said that if Dr. King were alive today, he would be appalled at the general condition of the black family and of affairs in the black community. He would rage against them with righteous disdain, like Moses did upon descending from the mountain and seeing the Israelites circled around the golden calf. That might be a good vignette for a cartoon version of our martyr, but Dr. King was not as spiritually and intellectually shallow as that. While he would lament the conditions, were he here, he would also understand them.

He would understand that while integration was a worthy goal, it also affected both black communal spirit and what a colleague of mine calls "black sodality."

Dr. King would understand the urge to reach for things that were previously denied, sometimes at the cost of communal and even filial bonds. He would understand that blacks, since the civil rights movement, have felt the need to create alternative cultures that were either cultures of resistance or cultures of identity, or both, separate and apart from the dominant Anglo culture so strongly associated with the former oppressor. He would understand that just as blacks are less equipped, after generations of oppression, to resist harmful social forces in general, they would be less equipped to resist the specific harmful social forces of materialism and consumerism. I think Dr. King would understand all of these things, even in the midst of his lamentations, and even as he prescribed solutions.

So do I. Love and understanding go together. Loving a people who have been so put-upon would seem to entail understanding, even compassion. While we may think that all of those horrible statistics about blacks shouldn't exist, we must face up to the fact that they do—not in spite of but because of a very peculiar history and social milieu, out of which neither blacks, nor whites, nor the nation as a whole have emerged. Not yet. Not entirely. So there is some distance left to travel before those statistics improve. There is no telling which forces and factors will end the entropy, turn the tide of failure, and begin the long journey toward success in the various ways success can be understood. It will come, in one way or another. In the meantime, what does love demand that we do?

That's hard to say when it is not clear what I mean by "we." Indeed, is there such a thing as "the black community"? Once, perhaps during King's or Garvey's days, that question would have been easy to answer. Black identity coalesced around such things as mere melanin, the black church (or the fatigue of the black church), resistance, the idea that you had to be twice as good as "them" if you wanted to make it, and a collective set of sensibilities about the world and how to engage it. Some of these survive, but many are fading, have faded.

As the intellectual pendulum swings away from even the notion of race (including whether there really are black and white races), the idea of a "we" becomes debatable. Are blacks even entitled to think of themselves as a "we," when the spirit of the times undercuts the concepts of static identities and melanin as *axis mundi* around which to gather or rally? Among the black middle classes, there seems to have always been at least *some* retreat from the idea of a black "we" that could be robust enough to encompass all of black identity. Education and money, however slowly it came, allowed the black middle class to entertain other possibilities.

Among the youth of the black working class and the black poor, another identity has been constructed to create sodality. And remember, understanding context is important. The context of that particular black identity includes hostility toward the values and sensibilities of the black middle class. By now, this is an old story—one that is not entirely true, but true enough. In rejecting some dimensions of the white/black/other middle class (certain habits, certain affectations, certain forms of speech, certain sensibilities), too many working-class blacks have also rejected (or have simply not come to value) many of the screws, nuts, and framing that hold the middle class in place—the very things that, in part, keep the middle class out of poverty, although sometimes just barely.

This is understandable. The resistance to certain middle-class values has its merits at times, Lord knows, even beyond the black community. Yet what tends to be classified as "middle-class values" does not *belong* to the middle class as such; in fact, they belong to all of us, if we want to employ them. When you hear an old man in a poor black neighborhood decrying the conduct of certain of his neighbors, he is expressing his commitment to those values. When you see a mother in a housing project chastising her daughter for misbehaving in school, she is expressing her commitment to those values. When you see a young boy on the subway trying to make sense of his *Scientific American*, he is expressing those values.

Middle-class values are no more than common sense, the application of reason to life's challenges, and the application of resolve to maintain the things that you hold dear and for which you have labored. They are not simply about affectation (although some-times, sadly, they are), but rather they are about *flourishing*. In too much of the black community, common sense has gone missing, not because rationality has gone missing, but rather because of the array of forces that serve to replace common sense with uncommon sense. Uncommon sense says that immediate gratification trumps deferred pleasure ("We real cool... We jazz June," in the immortal words of Gwendolyn Brooks); that rejecting Anglo values means one must reject values indiscriminately, the needless constraints that they are; that the whole structure of customs and norms that whites (and Asians and Brazilians and Nigerians, etc.) hold is all caught up in a way of being in the world that blacks can do without.

The fact is that *nobody* can do without them, and whites didn't invent them. The belief that they did is one of the terrible and toxic illusions that the African American community still suffers from, even if it is not acknowledged as such, even if it is not conscious. Such values are as old as the human brain. They are what keep the rich rich, and their absence has the doggedly persistent effect of keeping the poor poor. They help you cut through life's obstacles with greater ease, but their absence will leave you mired in the muck of human existence. Blacks know that this is no meritocracy, but persistence and credentials and mutual support can still kick open some doors.

No group of people can do well for long without stable homes, those incubators of the good friend, the solid citizen, the hero, the worthy spouse, even the good death. Just as we need to get beyond the notion that marriage is for white people, we need to also get beyond the notion that the incubator can be neglected. This doesn't mean that some blacks need to become overzealous toward family and home by walking around with an *f* for family on their chests or wear their commitment to home on their sleeves. It just means that in addition to considering all the things to be *avoided* in order to not become a statistic, we must consider the things that must be *present*, such as the important resources that a stable home provides.

An important key to changing black marriage (or stopping its de-cline) is for those blacks who give the home short shrift to think again, and then to make the home the center of the universe, even when home gets difficult. *It's supposed to be difficult.* It is one of the most important places in the world, and making it work is no easy thing.

The home, whether founded by straight or gay partners, is where life really happens. It does not need to be fancy or expensive, just as clean and as safe and as beautiful as you can make it. It is in the safety of the home that children's personalities blossom, just when you aren't looking. It is the place where a husband repledges, in the silence of the bedroom, to never touch another woman again as he watches his wife, who has given him so much, sleep in the soft light that sneaks in from the hallway. It is where you get the letter that Uncle James or Aunt Ruby has died, and where you all sit in a kind of circle and weep together, share memories, and feel shitty, and then go on to cook dinner and lay out your clothes for the next day.

Home is where the kids drive you insane in one instant, and make you laugh in the next. It's where you lay in bed at night holding hands and talking about your latest crisis of faith, or sobbing out your confessions, or singing oldies in the dark. It is the place where you are forgiven, and where you learn to forgive. It is what is left when there is nothing left, and it takes heart and hearts to keep it going. It's *worth* it. It makes everything else worth it, too.

I have learned all of this over my 26 years of marriage to my wife, my spouse, my life partner, Renee Osborne. We have had our setbacks, our painful times (some almost unbearable), the joys and sorrows that come with being together that long, with suffering through each other's changes. No doubt there is more to come. Is it worth it? Sometimes my heart tells me no. But my head always tells me, *yes, of course it is!*

And sometimes, when grace descends, my feelings and my head form a unity, and I know that life is only good because of the home that we have built, and that the really important things I have done in my life had nothing to do with building a business or getting a PhD or any other more or less solitary pursuit. All of the struggles to keep things on track have been worth it. And here's the thing—at some point along the way, when you least expect it, home is no longer the four walls that hold your bodies and your furniture. Home becomes a mystical thing that you can carry with you, that resides inside of you rather than you inside of it, and nothing can take it away from you, not even death.

When my sons Alex and Nick tell me that they love me and that they are grateful to have me as their dad, I can hear the voice of God speaking to me through them, and the other stuff I have done in my life pales. I know that if I were to drop dead right now, I have done my work. And no, it wasn't always easy, and I can still screw it up. But so far, so good.

I understand the statistics. If we want to change them, we need to rediscover the value of home, because home is where the action is. Its value and its promise transcend bling and fads and money. The bonds made there cannot only last a lifetime, but can create material, spiritual, and cultural wealth that can be passed down from one generation to the next, like bars of gold.

Saving marriage, whether in the black community or elsewhere, means coming to once again appreciate the value of home. And you don't need to be with someone, or in a relationship, to start thinking about that now. Home is not simply the place where you lay your head, eat your meals, and recover from illness. It is the place where you—working together with family—plant the seeds of love, life, and success into the bodies and the souls of those who dwell there and even, sometimes, into those who are just passing through; it is where those seeds are watered and fed so that what happens grows larger than the sum of the parts. Home is not a house or an apartment. It cannot be created alone. It is not a mere place; it is what happens there that makes it what it is. Two or more committed souls are the primary ingredients. Then comes the work. Can you be single and have a home? So long as it is a nexus of love and commitment, surely, that's why grandma's house is also home. It is the place where spirit lives, and to which spirit returns.

—**David E. McClean**

David E. McClean is a lecturer of philosophy, an ordained minister, a poet, and a business consultant. McClean teaches at Rutgers University in New Jersey and Molloy College in New York.

CHAPTER 9

The Best of Both Worlds

MY GRANDPARENTS, ROMUALD AND ELOISE HOWARD, WERE married for nearly 50 years. They were my first role models of what a healthy and loving relationship should be. Theirs was a very traditional relationship, with my grandfather being the provider for the household and my grandmother being the homemaker. They were very active grandparents who didn't live too far away, which meant that my brother, Paul, and I had the chance to spend time with them regularly. Looking back on my time with my grandparents makes me deeply appreciate the values and the confidence they instilled in us. They were a well-balanced couple who, even with life's challenges, were fiercely dedicated to their family.

When I went away to the University of Illinois to attend college, I met an ambitious, fun, and athletic guy through mutual friends. We fell for each other quickly, dated through college, eventually married, and had two wonderful sons. Because we met when we were 19 years old and married at 22, we essentially grew up together, navigating our way through young adulthood, figuring out how to be excellent parents, and traveling the world because of his career as a professional athlete. I was completely committed to my then-husband and our family, but I felt conflicted with what I wanted for myself. As a college-educated woman, I knew that I needed to be fulfilled professionally, and that was very difficult given the demands of his career. Eventually, it got to the point where I had to decide what I wanted for myself.

We spent a total of 18 years together, eventually going through a painful but necessary divorce in 2006. What I learned from our love, and our ultimate demise as a couple, is that the person you choose in your teens or twenties is sometimes very different from the person you would choose later in life. Your wants and needs change, and often people go off on different paths. So we had to make the adult decision that our marriage wasn't really working, but we've always been committed to providing our sons with a positive and loving environment.

The transition from a married woman (who had been married for a long time) to a divorcée was a challenge. First, I had to make sure that my kids were whole, since given their dad's schedule I was left carrying many of the parenting demands myself while he traveled for work. He played—and continues to play—a huge part in their lives, but a lot of the day-to-day was on me. I also had to figure out what to do with just myself as a woman.

For a long time after my divorce, I did not believe in marriage and I felt very firmly about that. Though I was juggling a demanding career and carried huge responsibility as a parent, my time as a single woman allowed me to be introspective. The time alone also allowed me to observe my friends and how they dealt with relationships. After taking a few years to assess my wants and needs, I realized that ultimately the experience of being single came up very short for me. I concluded that I really enjoyed having a partner in life.

In walked Ed, an incredibly handsome, self-assured, and well-dressed journalist who enthralled me with his intelligence, charm, and hazel eyes. Though we were both smitten with each other almost immediately, we kept our relationship on a professional level. Over time we developed a friendship, but we agreed to take our time to see how things developed. I expressed to him my doubts about the institution of marriage, but he completely changed my view. He is a very traditional man who enjoys being the head of the household, and I appreciate that. I know he's got my back and I've got his.

Ed and I have both been married before, so we knew what we wanted and also had a better understanding of how to make our relationship work. I'm still very much an independent woman, but I value what he brings to my life. He believes that communication is essential, and though I am known to be a little dramatic at times, he always makes sure that we talk things out and remind each other often that we're in this thing called love together. We each allow the other a voice in our relationship and the space to be who we need to be.

Our blended family moves so well together, with my two boys and Ed's daughter hitting it off right away. The kids took to each other immediately and they respect the fact that we make family time a priority in our household, and they look forward to that time. Of course there were some hurdles to overcome, but through it all our children have been in sync with Ed and me to make our new family unit work.

As for the future, Ed and I are building this family very well together—planning for the future to make sure that everyone's needs are being met, and that life is good for all of us. Within the context of our love for one another, I think I have finally found the best of both worlds—a happy, fulfilling marriage with the right partner and a solid career. For me, the second time around is oh, so good!

—Leslie Gordon

Leslie M. Gordon is a feature and entertainment writer with more than 22 years of strategic communications experience. Gordon is married to broadcast journalist Ed Gordon, and is the mother of three amazing children: Stephen, Taylor, and Landon. She is also an avid marathon runner.

CHAPTER 10

How I Met My Wife

Hollywood, California. Comedy Store. 11:34 p.m.

A lanky comedian walks briskly to the dimly lit stage, grabs the microphone, and then begins to spit out well-timed observations to the crowd. Two metrosexual friends are his initial targets, but then he casually turns and notices a smiling black couple nestled closely together and whispering to each other.

"Are we disturbing anything?" the comedian asks.

Laughter erupts from the crowd.

"Y'all need to get a room!" He loudly exclaims, then walks closer to the couple. "So where did y'all meet?"

"Las Vegas," the man answers.

"Las Vegas!?!" the comic hollers, "Y'all met in Las Vegas? Man, don't you know what happens in Vegas stays in Vegas?"

Fortunately for the couple, otherwise known as Vic and Jamila, that isn't what happened.

An Auspicious Introduction

If not for the eyes of one woman in particular, the two would've never met. After a night of partying with a group of buddies, Vic and a friend decided to break away from the pack and grab a quick bite at a diner inside the Hard Rock Hotel.

"Me and a friend were waiting in line to get into the diner and I heard someone calling my name," Vic explains. "I turned around and saw a sister sitting in a booth inside the restaurant, waving at me."

While his friend walked to their table, Vic strolled over to the woman. Her name was Tiffiani, an old friend with whom he'd lost contact years earlier. While Tiffiani and Vic caught up on each other's lives, his attention began to slowly turn toward Jamila.

"After me and Tiff talked for a minute," he says, "she introduced me to the two women sitting with her. It was late and I was really tired, but I couldn't stop thinking about how breathtakingly beautiful Jamila was. Her rich, dark skin tone. That smile. She was gorgeous, an aesthetic beauty in every sense of the word."

It wasn't Jamila's looks, though, that kept Vic's attention.

"I was really impressed with her career and interest in writing," Vic explains, "partly because most people don't mention writing as a hobby and I didn't expect that answer. I love to write, so when she said that, it sparked my interest. Jamila is gorgeous, but I'm from Los Angeles and you see attractive women all the time, so it's no big deal. Beautiful women with no substance don't impress me much. But it really was Jamila's intellect that made me want to get to know her better."

Jamila remembers the first meeting a bit differently.

"I thought he was extremely professional and forceful for some reason," Jamila recalls. "Not in a mean way, but he was abrupt. I just didn't think he was interested in me in that sense. I just thought he wanted to help me write, and wanted to extend himself to me. I thought, 'Wow, nice-looking guy and if he calls, wonderful.' But I didn't think he was going to follow up with me. We were in Vegas and it's just something you say to people to be cool like, 'Hey, we'll stay in touch' then never speak to them again. You just say it to be nice."

Piques Interest

Fast-forward to three days later, when Jamila was back in Southern California and received an unexpected call in the middle of the day.

"The first time Vic called me, I was so overwhelmed by his voice—very strong, confident, smooth," she says. "He asked me rapid questions; typical probably of his journalism background. He started out very professional and quickly asked if I went out during the week. We chatted and I realized in the first five minutes of our conversation that we had a great deal in common. I could tell that he wasn't running any lines, but that he dated a great deal, because again everything was very smooth. I did not want to get off the phone!"

Since the call was made while Vic was busy running errands, he had to eventually end it, but said that he would call back later. Of course, he didn't call that night. Jamila remembers that she "was a bit disappointed because I wanted to find out more about him. He called me at my office the next day and asked if we could get together for drinks after work. At first, I was a bit hesitant, but something told me not to play games. Plus, I was very curious."

An Unexpected Journey

The two agreed to meet at a local Red Lobster (Jamila: "I must admit, I was like *Red Lobster*???!!"), and on her drive there, Jamila spoke on her cell phone with Tiffiani.

"I told her that it was going to be a quick date," Jamila says. "I was going to eat, have a drink, talk a bit, and leave because I felt that Vic was asking me at the last minute! I was actually thinking about calling him and canceling, but Tiffiani told me that I was being silly and to just go. Usually, I would go home and get overly prepared for a first date, but I went straight from work! I got to the restaurant early and scoped out a great table. Usually first dates didn't make me nervous, but I was a bit anxious. When he finally arrived, I was already impressed. He was cute and clean-cut. I even remember his outfit: white button shirt, dark jeans. He was very cute and, I think, a bit nervous? Hmmm... I thought maybe this wouldn't be so bad! He grilled me on a couple of critical questions. It was a lighthearted banter back and forth; it was clear that he was smart, witty, charming and funny—and a bit gully!"

He told her his philosophy on how to treat special women in his life—with respect and devotion. Jamila also said that Vic seemed so different in his intensity.

"We ordered food, I picked the dish, and he cut my food for me!" she recalls. "It was so sweet. Vic then told me that I would be his wife someday. I was enjoying his humor throughout the date— so I was sure he was joking! I looked at him like he was crazy, but for some reason I didn't argue! I smiled and thought about it, maybe blushed a bit... We talked for hours and it was really easy and relaxing."

Jamila said that she didn't want to end the date, but it was getting late and the restaurant would soon be closing. Although the two didn't realize it at the time, they'd been talking and laughing for more than three hours.

"I felt like he was absorbing everything I said and that he was the type of man who would totally protect and nurture me," she says. "I could see myself lying in his arms all day talking, perfectly content. He walked me to my car and said that he would call me the next day. I came home extremely excited about my date—I even called Tiffiani and told her I was wrong. She said, 'I told you so...'"

Second Time Around

Several days later, Jamila was shopping at a mall when Vic called, saying that he had a surprise for her and wanted to connect during the upcoming weekend.

"I was very busy during this particular weekend," Jamila recalls, "but again, very curious to see him again and find out about the surprise. He picked me up the next day and we drove out to San Fernando Valley. I kept asking a lot of questions, but he wouldn't give out any information!"

The couple finally drove up to a large building (after getting lost), parked, and walked inside a massive recreation hall where Jamila discovered her unexpected surprise.

"It was a big band concert—mostly older crowd," she says. "Vic didn't wine and dine me; the venue only sold prepared lunches, so we had hot dogs and potato salad and watched an amazing performance. The music was beautiful and it was one of the best dates I have ever experienced. I mentioned that I loved big band music during our first date and he remembered!"

Vic explains it this way: "After our first date, I went online and searched for places that offered big band concerts in the area. None were scheduled to play at any of the 'cool' jazz clubs in town anytime soon. The only place was a Veterans of Foreign Wars post in the Valley. Soon as I saw the VFW logo, I knew it would be a much older crowd, but I felt that Jamila was open-minded enough to ignore the blandness of the venue and enjoy the music. I went with my gut and we ended up having a great time. She seemed to really love the show."

It was at the big band concert that Jamila knew Vic would always put the effort in to make her happy.

"After the concert," Jamila says, "he drove me back to my house and we had our first kiss! After he dropped me off, I went directly to the store and picked up my first bridal magazine ever. I have no idea why, it was only our second date... maybe subconsciously, I already knew?"

—Victor Everett

Vic Everett is an editor and writer based out of Los Angeles. He is the author of the book Six Easy Steps to Freelance Writing *and has also produced several direct-to-market film projects.*

CHAPTER 11

Being Patient

YOU KNOW THAT WOMAN WHO ALWAYS SEEMS TO HAVE A MAN? She can break up with her boyfriend on Tuesday and have four suitors by Friday? The girl who is in relationship after relationship, who never wants for a man's company?

I do too and I have always watched her in amazement, because she has lived the opposite existence of me. Though I've been called everything from cute to beautiful and have garnered my fair share of looks from the guys on the corner, dating has never been a simple affair for me.

I can count the boyfriends in my life on one hand, and I have often gone long stretches between relationships and, to be honest, even dates.

My romantic life seemed to mirror the dire statistics constantly thrown out about black women and their odds of having a life partner. Finding an eligible black man was hard enough. Finding an eligible black man who wanted a black woman was even harder, and then for that man to have the qualities one would want in a husband—the odds of marrying seemed insurmountable.

It's partly because of those hardships that I married young. My first husband (also my first boyfriend) was attractive, had a good job, had not one but three degrees, made me laugh, and seemed the marriageable type, and I did love him. Given the bleak prospects that black women are always told they have, why would I pass up a chance to avoid being another Unmarried?

Sometimes it's better to be alone than to be with a person who's not for you. And despite the many fine qualities of my first husband, our marriage was not a happy one, and I realized that he was just not the right person for me. I didn't know if a soul mate was real or existed for me, but at just 26, I had to at least try and find out.

When I left, my then-husband basically warned me that my chances of finding a soul mate were slim. I'll never forget him warning me that there weren't many black men out there who were marriage material, especially one as educated as he was. Would I really find someone better?

For many years, those words haunted me, and I worried he might be right. While I did have at least two serious relationships after that, I spent more time out of relationships than in them. (Surely, my own high standards were partly to blame: Taking my mother's advice, I never dated anyone I wouldn't consider marrying.) After my last relationship ended, in my mid-30s, I began to seriously wonder if my window for marriage had passed. Now I had to worry not only about that scary possibility, but also the bleak statistics of becoming a mother after the age of 35 (it never gets any easier, does it?).

It was in this time, when I was feeling hopeless, that I gained perhaps my greatest gift—my husband. It didn't start off perfectly. When we met, he was up front with me and told me he was dating different people. *Fine*, I thought. I can date other people, too (though realistically I had no options), and besides, we had just met!

But as my feelings for him deepened, so did the relationship with one of the other women he was dating, which struck me as a cruel, bitter irony. Here I had found a guy who I was so compatible with, who lived almost down the block from me, who wanted a relationship, but was seemingly not with me. I didn't know at the time that he was falling in love with me and that he was looking for a way out of that other relationship. I couldn't wait to see if he would end it. So I broke things off, and once again, was alone and, for a time, despondent.

But at some point, I had an epiphany: Whether I was alone or in a relationship, I had to hold the key to my own happiness. I might never get married. I might never be a mother. I might spend the rest of my life living with pets, watching my friends get married and celebrate anniversaries and Mother's Days. I could either deal with it in bitterness, or accept that God has another path for me, follow that path, and revel in the life that I had. Really, what was the other option? Being miserable?

So, on Valentine's Day 2008, while others were getting flowers, chocolates, and Victoria's Secret lingerie, I was at a romantic Dianne Reeves concert with two other women, both publicists (who both had their own men, by the way). It was a nice, work-related girl's night out, and I made sure I relished the moment. In the past, I might have been on the verge of tears contemplating what I was missing at that moment—most notably, a man. Instead, I realized I had great friends, a great job, an amazing family, great dogs, my own home, and an undoubtedly rich life. Not exactly what I wanted, but nothing to complain about either.

It was soon after that moment that the man who would become my husband called me. He told me he was no longer dating the other woman, and he wanted to be with me exclusively. A year and a half later, we were married.

While I believe that God was responsible for my fate, I also believe he delivered my husband to me at a time when I had come to accept my life for what it was, and be grateful for it. The doors opened for me once I stopped worrying about what was on the other side of it.

—Nekesa Moody

Nekesa Moody is the global entertainment and lifestyles editor for the Associated Press.

CHAPTER 12

Love on the Rocques

I WISH I COULD SAY IT WAS LOVE AT FIRST SIGHT, BUT THE ONLY L word that could describe how I felt when I first laid eyes on the woman who would eventually become my wife was *lust*. I was at a bar called Asylum down in the Village for my friend Will's 30th birthday party when I spotted Starrene walking by the window. Will and I were in the middle of a conversation, but as soon as I saw her it was like everything went in slow motion. My eyes stayed transfixed on her.

Starr was wearing a denim skirt and a form-fitting top that showed off all her curves, which she had in abundance. Her auburn locks were barely shoulder length at the time, but they were the perfect frame for her almond-shaped eyes and beautiful smile. The deep dimples in her mahogany skin only added to her cute factor. She was hot! Man, her MySpace pictures didn't do her justice.

Starr made her way through the crowd and over to where Will and I were seated. She greeted him first and then me: "Anslem, right?" Starr was working in PR at the time, and even though we had exchanged work-related emails and were MySpace friends, this was our first time meeting face-to-face. We wound up talking for the next half hour.

There was a definite connection between us, but I already knew she was taken based on her online relationship status—which could have just been a way to scare off the stalkers, but she mentioned her boyfriend in passing at least twice during our conversation. But I still got the sense that she was feeling me. It didn't matter, though, because I would never disrespect someone's relationship like that. So after that night we were in the friend zone.

Starr was 24 when we met and I was a few months shy of 30. As she was looking to break out of PR and into journalism, I became a mentor of sorts, on occasion offering up contacts, editor leads, and career advice. We were both night owls, and sometimes she would reach out to me about her career after hours. I thought that was odd for a woman in a relationship, but my ego just chalked it up to a girl with an innocent crush on an older man.

As the months went by, Starr and I maintained a strictly platonic relationship. It wasn't until after her relationship dissolved nine months later that we finally addressed the unspoken attraction that had been lingering beneath the surface from the start. We began hanging out more frequently and enjoyed each other's company for the next several months until I fell in love...

With someone else.

While Starr and I spent a lot of time together, there was never a conversation about exclusivity. I'm not sure if she exercised her option to see other people, but I certainly did. I was a career bachelor with a penchant for disappearing, and it was during these gaps in time that I would go out with other women. Although Starr and I had a strong connection, due to our age difference I never took her seriously as someone I could be with in a long-term relationship.

It wasn't intentional, but another woman captured my heart. Telling Starr wasn't something I was looking forward to, but it had to be done. I had to explore the feelings I had for this other woman, and if the relationship had any shot at working I couldn't have any distractions. So on a mild October night, I took Starr to a barbecue restaurant near Madison Square Garden to break the news (and break her heart) over buffalo wings and margaritas.

After almost a decade of being single, I was finally ready to commit—just not to the woman sitting across from me. It was a tough pill for Starr to swallow, but she had no choice in the matter. I didn't want to hurt her, as we'd shared many great moments, but I had to listen to my heart. It was telling me that I needed to take a shot at love in another woman's arms.

We can't help who we fall in love with or when. Starr learned that the hard way, and eventually I did as well. After several months of courtship, my new relationship came to a head. As much as I cared for this new woman, the fact was we came from completely different backgrounds and our lifestyles didn't mesh together as seamlessly as I had imagined. As quickly as my love affair started, it came to an abrupt end.

I was heartbroken.

It's always a blow to the ego when someone you really care about rejects you. In the wake of the breakup, I found myself in an emotional slump. I threw myself back in the dating ring to distract myself from my feelings, but I wasn't in the right frame of mind to give anyone my undivided attention. I existed as a fractured soul, floating from place to place, until fate intervened.

After months of trying to break into publishing, Starr finally landed an entry-level position at a major music magazine. It was her dream job, but of all the mags in the world, why'd she have to get a job at mine? It was awkward, to say the least. Though we were cordial to each other following our split, Starr and I hadn't really seen each other since that fateful night back in October.

Luckily, Starr and I didn't have to interact directly in the office. When we did, she'd usually keep it short, sweet, and to the point. It was obvious she was still hurting about how things ended between us, and I can't say that I didn't feel guilty about it, too. During the time that she and I went out, we never had an argument; we got along great, and there was amazing chemistry between us. I was just too concerned about her age to appreciate the experiences and the woman while I had the chance.

Going from no contact at all to seeing Starr every day was torture. She was still sexy as hell, and every time I was in her presence I was reminded of that fact. I caught myself quite a few times staring at her across the conference room table during staff meetings, or watching her hips sway as she walked down the hall. I wish I could say love was finally on my mind, but this was still all about that other L word.

I tried to be a better man by keeping my distance, but that's hard to do when the person you're trying to avoid sits three cubicles over. Then, someone got the bright idea that I should be Starr's editor for the magazine's new film and TV section. Forced to work with me, Starr slowly ended the cold-shoulder treatment and warmed up to the idea of us being friends again. Regardless of how things ended, we were always able to talk effortlessly, and working together helped us fall back into a familiar space. Going over story ideas during work hours led to hanging out after work and, eventually, we found ourselves back in this undefined gray area.

Mixing business with pleasure wasn't something we'd planned, but there was this unexplainable energy that kept drawing us together. Still, the idea of being involved with someone at work made me nervous. Worried about people finding out or having the relationship negatively affect our careers, I tried to keep our outer-office mingling to a minimum, which made me come off like a jerk. One minute I'd be hot, and the next I'd be cold. I was fighting my emotions at every turn, and the uncertainty frustrated Starr. I was a grown man who didn't know what he wanted. I enjoyed spending time with Starr, but as long as we worked together, I couldn't let my guard down and just let go.

I didn't have to worry about that for long, as the Great Recession took care of that for us. After a year of working side by side, Starr and I both got laid off on the same day. Not for secretly dating as I had always feared, but because of budget cuts. With the pressure of fraternizing with a coworker now gone, we were finally able to actually work on us.

It felt right, but a part of me was still scared. I had no problem going with the flow, but after the way things ended the last time and seeing that hurt look in Starr's eyes, I knew I couldn't take her down that path again. I couldn't string her along again, so my only options were to let her go for her own good or actually give us a chance. After some soul searching and really analyzing the woman Starr had transformed into, I made my decision. I just prayed it was the right one.

They say a criminal always returns to the scene of the crime. I guess that's why I asked Starr to meet me on Thirty-Fourth Street for dinner. We walked through the crowded Midtown streets and made our way back to the same barbecue spot from a year and a half earlier. A look of familiarity filled Starr's eyes as we approached the restaurant, but she didn't say a word.

Once seated, we placed our order, and I struck up a conversation as if the place didn't hold bad memories for us. When we were halfway through our meal, I put my knife and fork to the side and addressed the proverbial pink elephant in the room.

"Do you remember this place?" I began.

"Yeah," Starr replied with a look that was part quizzical, part annoyed.

"Well, the last time we were here I made a really big mistake that hurt you, so I brought you back here tonight to make up for that. Over the past year and a half, I feel like we've both changed a lot. I know we fell out of touch for a bit, and that's my fault, but I'm glad that we were able to get back on track. I just don't want to hurt you like I did last time, so I've decided that I'm ready. I love you, and if you'll have me, I want you to be my girl for real. I want to give us a shot."

It took her a minute to process what I was saying, but once she did, Starr smiled and said, "Yes."

Over the next two years, our relationship evolved organically. Completely committed to each other, we dated exclusively and spent all our free moments together. After extended sleepovers at my place, I gave Starr a key so she could come and go as she pleased, but she never left. The truth is that I didn't want her to. Starr officially moved in, and we were happy, but I soon found myself at another emotional crossroads.

Going into 2011, I was reflective about my future. By year's end, I would be 35. If there was such a thing as a male biological clock, mine would surely be ticking soon if it hadn't started already. Starr had been a part of my life, off and on, for the past four years; if she wasn't The One, then I was just wasting time—hers and mine.

I'd already given up my decade-long run as a bachelor for a committed relationship that worked effortlessly, so there was only one step left to take, right? But was I really ready for *that* L word? Making it legal? Like most men, I was unsure. Of course I loved Starr with all my heart, but marriage was the ultimate step. It wasn't something that could be decided on a whim or "just because." I not only had to make sure I was ready emotionally, but also that she was The One I could see myself with forever.

I had to think on it.

I spent the rest of the year weighing the pros and cons of my relationship with Starr. She made me happy but was far from perfect. Like me, she had flaws, but I learned that choosing a life partner isn't about finding perfection; it's about knowing the difference between what you want and what you need. You have to be willing to compromise some of the things on your long list of ideals and key in on the qualities that matter most to your happiness.

The more I thought about it, the less I found wrong with Starr. Age was just an excuse at this point, and if that was the only "problem" I had with her, then I was a bigger fool than she thought I was when I called it off years earlier. Still, making that leap of faith on love is scary and I wasn't sure if I was ready. I needed more time to mull it over—until that switch just flipped.

We were sitting in our living room trying to figure out where to go for our summer vacation when it finally hit me that Starr was The One. I wasn't sure which one of us suggested it, but St. Lucia came up as a possible destination.

"Let's go to St. Lucia," I blurted out. "Book the tickets."

As soon as the words left my mouth, I knew I was ready to marry Starr. My mother was from St. Lucia, and I hadn't been back there since I was five years old. It seemed like the perfect place to pop the question. It just made sense to start my new family in the place where my family was from. I didn't care how much the tickets cost. My mind was set, and there were no more doubts. Okay, maybe one or two, but the more thought I put into it, the more at ease I felt with my decision and the prospect of our future together.

I spent the next few weeks talking to an already-married friend about where to get a ring. After visiting a few stores he suggested and looking online, I finally settled on a jeweler near my job. For the next three months, he walked me through the process of designing Starr's ring. Although I didn't know the first thing about jewelry, I knew Starr and I wanted to get her something that reflected her quirky personality. The end product was just that: a one-of-a-kind ring crafted with her in mind.

St. Lucia was beautiful. The trip was just what Starr and I needed, a break from the stresses of New York and the perfect destination to just relax and enjoy each other's company. We hit the beach often and explored the exotic locales of my homeland, even visiting the house where my mother grew up. It was here, among the spirit of my ancestors, that all doubt completely washed away. On what was to be our last night in St. Lucia, I took Starr for a moonlit stroll on the beach after dinner. There, on the beach, I dropped to one knee and asked her the most important question a man could ever ask a woman.

She said yes.

Although she had no clue I was going to propose, Starr was ready and so was I. We were so sure about getting married that we didn't see a need for a long engagement. Neither of us wanted to go another year as singles. We initially toyed with the idea of a December wedding so we could go into 2012 as husband and wife, but with Christmas and my birthday the day after, it just didn't make sense logistically. Starr started plotting January dates and originally picked the 21st, but a week later, something told her to push the wedding up to the 14th. We locked in a venue for that date a month later and I thought nothing of it. It wasn't until a few weeks later that I realized the significance of that date.

I was on the phone with my mother one Sunday morning, updating her on the wedding plans, when she nonchalantly said, "You know the 14th was the day Grandpa was buried, right?" In the midst of all the planning, it had totally skipped my mind that January 11th was the anniversary of my grandfather's passing, and that this year would mark 25 years. I took the fact that of all the dates on the calendar, Starr chose the 14th—the same day he was buried—as a sign that our marriage was meant to be.

My grandfather was the only father figure I had known, and since there was no one left to carry on his name, I had decided a few years back to change my name to his. My plan had always been to wait until I got married to legally change my name along with my wife, assuming she would want to bear my last name. Thankfully, Starr was more than willing to share in my tribute to my grandfather. So on the morning of January 14, 2012, we, the couple formerly known as Anslem Samuel and Starrene Rhett, resurrected my grandfather's name and were rechristened Mr. and Mrs. Rocque.

Without a doubt, our path to the altar was far from easy, but neither of us would trade any of the bumps along the way for the payoff we received: each other. I needed to grow into the man Starr deserved, and she had to be strong enough to accept me, flaws and all. Most women wouldn't have given me a second shot after all the heartache I put her through, but true love makes you do things you never thought you would because it just feels right. I wish I could say it was love at first sight, but if it had been, we wouldn't have had the same appreciation for each other and the journey we took to reach our Happily Ever After.

—Anslem Samuel Rocque

Anslem Samuel Rocque has been a music and entertainment journalist for more than 14 years and has held editorial positions at notable media publications ranging from the Source *and* XXL *to* Black Enterprise *and the* Ave, *where he served as the founding editor-in-chief. In addition to his work appearing in mainstream print and online outlets, Rocque is the creator of the award-winning relationship blog Naked With Socks On, and co-creator of TheLoversRocque.com, where he and his wife, Starrene, muse about the inner workings of a marriage in progress.*

CHAPTER 13

The Power of Adapting

I WANT WOMEN TO BE ENCOURAGED WHEN THEY ARE IN relationships. Don't sabotage your own happiness. I think a lot of women—especially when they've been single for a long time—don't even know they're sabotaging themselves. They're coming in expecting too much from their man. And men run from that. They do.

So you're like, "How did this chick over here, who doesn't have anything going for herself, end up with a man like that? I have a college degree, my own house, and I'm doing this and that, but I can't get a man?" It's because you're too power hungry. You're used to running things yourself. You've got to back all that down so he can be the man. Men need to feel like they can be the man.

You shouldn't settle, but don't expect the moon and the stars, because you're not going to get them. I think a lot of times women expect men or a marriage to complete them, and that's exactly the total opposite of reality. When you sign on that dotted line and you say "I do," you're committing to a job. It's work. And you're only rewarded for the work that you put in.

And then, people don't get this: The ego has to go. It's impossible for people to stay married with egos. I think that's why we see a lot of breakups—in Hollywood, especially, in marriages with two powerful people whose egos eventually clash and consume what was supposed to be magical and last forever. There is only so long that you can suppress those egos.

I'm sure there are women who look at me and think that I have the perfect life. But they don't see the tears. They don't see all the praying and they don't see the stuff that goes into making it work.

Marriage alone requires a lot of work. If you don't already have a solid relationship, kids can throw a serious wrench into the situation. My husband Anthony and I had been married for five years when the twins came along—we celebrated our seventh wedding anniversary recently—and that was a long time to be together. All told, we've been together for nine years. If we had had our kids sooner, I'm not sure how our relationship would have turned out.

What has gotten us through is trusting and knowing that even though it's not perfect, we aren't going to leave each other. I did go through some fear and insecurity—especially when I was pregnant, which nobody could prepare me for. Nobody really talks about how insecure you feel about your body during and after pregnancy, when your body has been stretched out and looks different. You don't have that young, beautiful body anymore. On top of that, Anthony's a celebrity, and women are constantly throwing themselves at him, which of course makes things even more challenging for us.

After the twins were born, the time that we would have given to each other was devoted to them. So we ended up doing the exact thing we said we wouldn't do—we neglected each other. Sometimes because you're giving so much to the kids, you find yourself too tired to put in the effort. He's a very hands-on dad, which was taxing. He wanted to do things his way, and I wanted to do them my way, so we found ourselves arguing more than agreeing.

Raising the kids is just another element of marriage that you have to debate and come to an agreement on. What they wear, what toys we buy—every single thing is a decision. But as they've gotten older, we've learned to choose our battles. We find ourselves parenting them together now instead of parenting them separately. I think I give in a lot more. I allow Anthony to do things the way he wants to. I think I used to put up a fight more, wanting to control a little bit more of what goes on with the twins.

My marriage could have easily taken a fall because at first, I struggled with keeping my career as an artist. I ended up resenting my husband because I felt I was stuck at home with the children. If I'd kept that attitude, I would have ended up losing because I wasn't stepping up to my responsibilities at home. I had to consider what made sense for us. He had already reached celebrity status and was the principal breadwinner. Why should he sacrifice everything he'd worked for just so I could have a job?

What I've come to realize is that I am a part of his success, because my presence allows him to go out and tour with peace of mind, knowing his family is taken care of and that the children are being loved by their mother. I've made our house a home. It's beautiful and peaceful, and wherever he is, he knows he has that waiting for him. I'm a part of this machine. I'm a part of all this working, and that's the big picture.

This doesn't mean that because I'm not bringing in money myself I'm not working. This doesn't mean that I don't have any value here. It took me becoming a mother to really get that. And now I feel valuable. I know that I'm priceless. I feel like I'm worth more, and it makes me even more confident to know he'll never find anybody else like me, ever. I always used to say that, but now I know that for sure. Nobody else could have given him these beautiful babies, with these characteristics, with these talents we already see. He couldn't have done this with anybody else but me. And so that's what I ride on.

I'm part of a blended family with Anthony, and my biggest challenge was being too involved sometimes. I would really take to heart the things that would go on with his older boys. The two older ones pretty much lived with us, so I helped rear them when they were in high school.

It worked out because I became a confidante for the boys. They would come and talk to me about things that they didn't feel comfortable talking to their dad or mom about. I would share those things and try to translate them to their parents so that they were able to communicate better. It's hard for a teenager to communicate with his parents, and vice versa. Having an intermediary helps, and that's what I was to them.

It was never an issue of, "You're always trying to spend time with your kids and I want you to myself." It was never that. It was always me wanting to include the kids. And we would go at it because I would tell him, "I think you should discipline them this way concerning an issue," or I'd say that he didn't do enough. Sometimes, he would say, "Would you just back off? They have a mom and a dad." A lot of times, my little feelings would get hurt. I used to hate that I cared so much.

But I'm rewarded with two good boys who love me. They're crazy about me. One of them calls me Mama Two because he doesn't like calling me by my first name. They consider me their second mom today, so my overinvolvement was worth it.

I think our story would have been different if he had girls. And I always tell him that. Girls are different, and to them I would have been another woman coming in, sharing their dad's attention. Girls can be something else. I think I got it easy with him having all boys because it never felt like, "She's in the way." And I really tried to be welcoming to them. I respected them first. I didn't come in saying, "Respect me because I'm the adult," because I wasn't old enough to be their mother.

I knew I was coming into a fragile situation. My parents are divorced, so I know what that feels like when there is somebody else, a boyfriend or a girlfriend, coming around. They need to see that you respect them, and that you respect their space, so that's what I chose to do. Through my actions, I earned their respect, trust, and love.

Family is very important to me in all aspects, including the tough issues. We've got to heal these wounds because life is too short, and I don't want to have those regrets. When we got married, I told him that I thought it was important he reconnect with his biological father, who is still alive and lives nearby. I told him that no matter what had gone on before, as long as his dad was alive, there was room for forgiveness and reconciliation.

I think you have to let your parents know how you feel. Get it out and move on. I think it has made Anthony a better dad to let go of his anger and not have bad feelings against his parents or anybody else. There's nothing worse than still wanting to ask questions of a person who is already in his grave. You can't get closure. Anthony really took that to heart. He even sings about it, in "I Know What Love's All About." The song's lyrics reveal, "I'm friends with my old man, pretty much because of you." They still keep in touch to this day.

I think he helps teach me a lot about myself, too. I used to be really hard on him and always try to pass judgment, like, "You should be doing things this way if you're supposed to be a Christian." I was trying to strongarm him, and he would behave as I wanted him to for a little while. Then he would rebel, saying, "No, I want to be who I am."

It taught me a lot about myself. I realized that following all the rules I learned in my strict church upbringing doesn't make a person a Christian. Anthony helped bring that to light for me, saying, "Look, you're passing judgment on me, but what about you?" It helped me look at myself, too, because I'm not perfect. He was the first person to really challenge me to do that.

I always go back to my relationship with God. My faith has a lot to do with why I'm able to tough things out. I have a God who constantly forgives me. He never turns away from me. He still loves me unconditionally. I can always go back and say, *I'm sorry, I know I messed up, I did it wrong—again.* And I can feel that I have that peace, that presence of God, knowing that He hasn't left me. If God hasn't left me, how can I leave Anthony?

I think loss also has a lot to do with it. When you've seen death, experienced watching a person leave this earth, you realize how fragile we are as people, and what sort of time we have here. Compared to eternity, eighty or ninety years of my life here on earth is not a long time. I know that I don't have much time with Anthony here on earth—because even if we're married fifty years, to me, that's not a lot of time.

All in all, I think our relationship has lasted because there's been a lot of patience and a genuine love. Not the commercial love that people see, not the temporary love, but the love that the Bible speaks of. A love that when everything else fails and everything else is gone, the love still stands. And I have that type of love for him. I've never loved anybody like I love him.

—**Tarsha' Hamilton**

Tarsha' Hamilton is a woman who wears many hats. She is a singer/songwriter who has traveled to many parts of the country and the world sharing her gift. She also speaks boldly as an advocate for those affected by HIV/AIDS, participating with various organizations to break the silence about the disease. Married to R&B superstar Anthony Hamilton, she is a wife and mother who is enjoying the experience of raising three small boys in the balance she calls life.

CHAPTER 14

Marriage Is Grand—A Fine Institution

FOR A LOT OF CATS, MARRIAGE IS AN UNDISCOVERED COUNTRY. When people get to know me and find out that I was married once, they gather at my feet like I'm some wise old tree. It's as if they don't get the main thing: that it's over, and it wasn't a success by any definition. Still, they want to know what I learned, and they insist on all the macabre marital minutiae I can muster.

All the guys I know are always talking about what bitches their ex-wives are. Not me, Jack. My ex-wife was and remains a quality individual. Most times, I don't admit to knowing her, much less having married her. When people insist that I give up my ex-wife's identity, I tell them I married one of the Muppets, which is probably closer to the truth.

But then here you are, you who wants to know about love and marriage. Well, just know, as you gather 'round, that aside from any novella and subsequent film on the matter (hint hint), this is the last time I want to talk about my ex. It's just a rehash... a bad rehash, at that. And given that she has declined to make her side public, it seems unfair for me to write about it much more. Perhaps you, and the subject of marriage itself, are best served with a list of lessons rather than the sordid, bloody detail. So gather 'round, and dodge the spittle, as I lay it down.

The first lesson I learned about marriage I actually learned while my ex and I were dating: Always trust your instincts. When I met my ex, she was free—she had a fuck buddy, but nobody staking a claim—and that should have tipped me off immediately. Why is this fine, intelligent black woman virtually alone? Some folks are alone by choice, and that's cool for you, because then you can tell right up front they're sick. No normal person, given a choice, wants to live life alone—that's a life of Ex-Lax, multiple cats, and *Matlock*. People are normally alone because they're fucked up and nobody can deal with that shit for longer than it takes to bust a nut, get dressed, and leave. As it happens, when I met my ex, I was already occupied, and that isn't uncommon. Anyone with anything to offer at all already has someone trying to stake a claim. Not that I was the bomb catch, by any stretch... but I had certain charms that discerning women covet.

Second lesson I learned: Recognize girls with more game than you. I thought my ex was a suburbanite who couldn't compete with my club-tested, ghetto-approved street legalese. I don't know how I could have been so wrong. My ex was sophisticated, a player in her own right, with an internationally known type A rep. She fronted like a rookie, but was clearly a pro—she disarmed me very, very quickly, and it wasn't long until I followed her like the sun follows the storm: slowly and without question. I mean, very early on, I was in love.

I know because I'd been around it a bit. I mean, love had come and left, and love and I went to the same parties and danced at all the same clubs; we'd even shared cocktails after hours. I knew love well. I'd been smitten and bitten by a woman before and come out on top, so meeting someone and falling in love wasn't going to happen. Not to me. Not while I was awake. But it happened like a weather event, and took me under in short order.

The third lesson I have learned is: Love don't pay the rent or fire ambitions. What do I mean? Well, my ex and I started out as a bus-stop couple—brokeity-broke—and got married in much the same way. Financially, we had come from two different black cultures: I had been raised more or less in a state of near-poverty, but she had the idea (whether real or imagined) that she was from some tony middle-class background. Really, our backgrounds were similar, but that gap in perception caused us to have a different way of dealing with our circumstances.

While I'm kind of a survivalist, willing to sacrifice for the greater good and a common goal, she may not have been as willing to commit to some of those sacrifices. We both agreed to help each other through undergrad, and we both acknowledged it'd be uncomfortable, a struggle, like it's supposed to be. But to me, struggling meant having no food; for her, it meant basic cable. These doldrums were just par for me, because I knew it was temporary and that I would blow up one day…for something.

So my mistake was two-fold: While poverty and ambition have their own distinct romanticism, and there is nothing sweeter than starting at the bottom and ending up on top, not everyone is feeling that approach. Some dreamer chicks wanna come out the gate ballin', and expect the man to sustain that vision of the good life, whatever the cost to his wallet or his personal agenda. So not only was I broke, I was ambitious. Sometimes people have their own agendas, and your ambition may get in the way. My ex found a way to fix that.

The next lesson was learned the hard way, so peep game: For reasons that are still unexplained, my ex became indescribably, torturously abusive. I say that because I know how hard it is for some people to get their heads around the idea that a woman can physically abuse a man, particularly a 5-foot-10, 200-pound (give or take) brother who has seen many a street fight and lost nary a one.

The idea must strike you as funny. I'll spare you her weight and measure, but I assure you this young lady destroyed me from the inside out. The punani deprivation and browbeating had me bent the fuck up, losing all consideration for anything that didn't benefit her, including my future. I would put her first, and she would take care of me on the other end, she said. The public and private emotional abuse would have probably been sufficient, but the physical abuse completed the trifecta of humiliation and added a unique element of degradation. And who's gonna believe me when I tell them this story?

Nobody, as it turned out. I asked her moms and her clergy for assistance, and they told me to "handle it the best way" I knew how—probably the stupidest fuckin' advice I've heard in such dire and potentially dangerous circumstances. Why a woman in her right mind would raise her hand to any man, barring self-defense, baffles me. While it should be said that I was no prize, I never, ever raised my hand unless I was fending off assaults from hands, fists, or household cleaning agents.

Now I know I said I asked her moms for some advice, and that's true. That's just because her pops wasn't around, and I was desperate. As an aside, I can stress the importance of keeping moms out of your business. Her moms got all sorts of advice—no man and no prospects, but all sorts of advice. Nip that in the bud as quickly and as decisively as possible. If not, you'll be stuttering now and for eternity. Respect her moms? Absolutely. But respect is a two-way street. Live it. Learn it. But I digress.

After bullying me out of some of my money-market account, she paid a school debt, went back to school, busted her ass, and graduated. I dropped out and tried to generate some bread for the household, confident that she was going to hold up her end of the deal and help me through school. I reminded her that it was my turn to concentrate on school. She balked. HARD.

"I don't think so," she said.

She bounced two months later. Meanwhile, I'm sitting there, broke, school debt of my own, no woman, no job, and no prospects. The lesson? Nice guys finish last and die hard, Jack: That's the next lesson, and take it to the grave, son. People mistake kindness for weakness on the regular, and will roll you like a dead dog if they see an opportunity.

Marriage is a fine institution. Like Rikers.

One of the last conversations we had was about how I didn't deserve to go to college, that I wasn't smart enough, and what did I think I wanted to be anyway?

"Well," I said sheepishly, "I was thinking advertising... but now I dunno. I think I want to be a journalist... a writer."

"A writer?!" she said. "Listen, you'd *better* be trying to get a job at a factory or something, because you will never, *ever*, be a writer. There aren't many things you could do, and trust me, writing is not one of them."

The irony is delicious, isn't it?

It seemed to me that the minute—the *minute*—she was out of my life, everything and everyone started to change, and that's true.

I handled my business and became not just a writer, but a respected print and online journalist with an international byline. Next stop: books, TV, movies, even? Nah, for now I have to pick up some diapers for my newborn and buy a *Times* for my girl, who stays at home because she doesn't have to work. She's weighing her options from the comfort of our four-bedroom, two-bath condo on the East Side.

My ex and I live in the same city, but we only speak when obligated, and she doesn't feel obligated, so lately I don't either. All that hassle and hustle about getting a degree, and she is largely doing what she was doing when she left. We were committed to shaking up the world, and that was the best she could do. Honestly, I pity her, in the way that you pity ugly rich people. It's just so pathetic. I used to really want her friendship, but there again she tried to hustle me. So now I don't give a fuck anymore. I don't study it too much. It hurts still, at times, and there remain so many questions. But Tajah is warming up the PS2, Mr. Chuckles is expecting his daddy, and my lady is cooking all my favorite foods…

———————

When my girl and I met, I had no ride, no idea how to drive, and no desire to learn anytime soon. I'd been traumatized by a couple of car accidents, and the bus-ems was good enough for me, Jack. Slow, but sure. Believe it or not, it wasn't the worst thing in the world, because it afforded us a lot of time to talk and get to know each other, which is the ideal way to exploit this circumstance. I know brothers try to romanticize poverty and bus love, and that just ain't gonna work.

Fact is, I don't know if what I know about love and marriage is that new or different. But I don't mind telling you what I know.

When we first got married, it was Kool and the Gang…kinda.

Some things are gonna shoot you right in the foot. Marrying a woman who can't cook is like asking for a life of takeout and pizza delivery men, and the bills and calories that come with that. Ask her to just shoot you now, before the cholesterol and the dinner checks take you under. Sure, you could learn how to cook, but what the hell is she there for anyway?

You think there are some things that you don't *want* to know about her? Well, get your mind around this: She farts, man—she farts *loud*. So loud you'll duck. And sometimes, your toilet will reject your lady's turds, logs so big they could torpedo a U-boat. She doesn't always smell like Chanel No. 5, but then neither do you, Musty McCrusty—welcome to intimacy.

Moms always has an opinion. Your moms and hers. Making sure your moms knows her place should already be a foregone conclusion, but man, keep her moms out of your business. That's rule number one, really. Nothing will poison your relationship quicker than the Mother-in-Law Blues. Respect her moms? Absolutely. But respect is a two-way street, and it sometimes means knowing your boundaries.

—Jimi Izrael

Jimi Izrael is a writer, NPR contributor, and academic originally from the suburb of East Cleveland, Ohio.

CHAPTER 15

It's Not Where You're from... It's Where You're at

I GREW UP IN A TIME WHEN RESTROOMS WERE CLEARLY MARKED "Colored." I grew up in a time when you didn't dare look a white person in the eye. I grew up in a time when a visit to town meant hopping in a buggy tied to the back of a horse. I grew up in a time when paved roads were a luxury. And there wasn't a television or a telephone in sight.

I grew up in a little community called Mount Olive in the backwoods of Mississippi. My state was consistently listed as the poorest in the nation, a state where Jim Crow lived and thrived for decades. And right smack in the middle of it is a tiny rural town tucked in the woods called Lexington, a predominantly African-American town with a population of less than 1,000 in the 1950s. Gravel roads led up to the doorstep of my home, which my grandfather, nicknamed Big Cotton, built with his bare hands. My nearest neighbor was miles away.

I lived on a farm with Big Cotton, who was a deacon at the church, and my grandmother, Ms. Bookie, who could scare away the devil just by the glare in her eye. She was a tough, no-nonsense woman. And when she reached for that switch, belt, or shoe... I felt she was Lucifer himself.

Our farm was robust. We owned horses, chickens, roosters, pigs, dogs—you name it. During the summer I had to pick cotton under the hot, sweltering sun. And in the winter, I chopped wood for the fire. I was only seven years old when I started as a waterboy (yes, *boy* is what they called me). I had to tie a jug of water to my tiny body and walk through the fields quenching the thirst of the adult cotton pickers. By the time I was eight, I graduated from waterboy to gathering the crops from the farm myself—the corn, peanuts, and sweet potatoes. I even milked the cows, and fed the hogs... and later on, I had to kill the hogs.

There was no task too large for my little frame. While it was a tough life for a kid, it taught me hard lessons I would never forget. Most importantly, a lot of what I learned on the farm came from watching my grandmother and grandfather's committed relationship. They were two spirit-filled people who believed strongly in God and provided for their family. We went to church every Sunday, and I dared not get my Sunday dress or shoes dirty.

Like a lot of others in Mississippi, we didn't have much. I always shared a bedroom with my sisters and brothers. For our birthday or Christmas, we would only get one gift apiece. There was no extra spending, no Friday night dinners at the local diner, and no frills at all.

I was the youngest of six siblings. Each of them left Mississippi after they graduated high school. They headed north and west: Chicago, California, and Detroit. Back then, that was just the way it was—after you graduated, you left home. My oldest sister was ten years older, so she left when I was only eight. Then slowly, one by one, they each made their way to what I called "Mississippi North" and left me all alone.

By the ninth grade, not only did I have to take care of the farm but I had to take care of my grandmother as well. She had had several strokes that left her semi-mobile and totally dependent on me. As the only child left in the home, I was responsible for cleaning the house and washing the clothes (which at that time meant going out back and washing them by hand on a wash board, then hanging them on the line to dry). I had to cook all the meals for the family. I couldn't go anywhere or enjoy any teenage activities. My grandmother was so sick and so strict that I wasn't allowed to do anything but take care of her. Yet somehow she was never too sick to whip me.

I remember one night wanting desperately to attend a party at the local juke joint. I asked my grandmother and of course she said no! So I decided I was going away. I hid my clothes in the outhouse. (Yes, we had outdoor plumbing.) I tucked my party clothes behind the commode. After dinner, I asked to go to the restroom. I slipped out the back door, and down to the outhouse. I quickly changed into my outfit and I was ready for the night. Once I was all gussied up, I ran like Forrest Gump! Like Kunta Kinte! I ran so far and so fast that I was out of breath by the time I arrived at my friend Geraldine's house.

Geraldine and I hitched a ride to the nearby juke joint, called the Village. I partied so hard that night, I thought it was 1999 long before Prince ever did! Well, it was for me—the end of the world, that is. I knew that my life would be over once my grandmother realized that I was missing. So I did the twist, the funky chicken, the dog, the boogaloo, and the swing like never before. I figured if I was going to die, I might as well have a blast before I go. And sure enough, when the fun was over, I had to drag myself back home. It was around midnight, pitch dark in the woods. I snuck in the house and climbed into bed. But I was smart. I padded myself with a big old quilt because I knew my grandmother would be in shortly. And as sure as the sky is blue, minutes later my grandmother dragged herself into my room and beat the crap out of me with a stick. The next day, I woke up... I was alive! Everything was back to normal.

My grandmother was extremely mean, and if I did anything wrong, I would get hit across the nose, head, face, mouth, arm, or wherever she could grab me. In high school, she made me transfer to a private school because she thought I was "getting too fast" at my school. I remember it like it was yesterday. We had to wear these long, blue skirts with light blue blouses. I hated it. My grandmother made a young man drive me to school every day to keep me out of trouble. He made me sick! He was always watching over me and acting like my father (little did I know, I would end up marrying him).

For my senior prom, my grandmother picked my date and made my uncle drive us and bring us right back home. Yes, it was rough growing up: no texting, no computers, no phones, no vacations, no hanging out, no visiting the malls or going to movies, no extracurricular activities... nothing! As you can probably imagine, I resented my grandmother for not letting me have a childhood.

Finally, I was old enough to leave. I moved to Chicago in 1968 to live with my mother. It took me a while to realize my mother was really my mom. Being raised by my grandparents, I always thought that my grandmother was my mother. But every summer, a really nice lady would come visit me. She was very pretty and very nice, and she would always bring such nice gifts. The only thing I didn't like is that she would bring this little prissy girl with her every time. I had to wait on her hand and foot. It reminds me of *The Color Purple* where Miss Celie always had to wait on the prissy drunken Shug. I hated that little girl, but I played with her. It took me about ten years to realize that the woman who visited every summer was the woman who gave birth to me.

To this day, I'm not quite sure why my mother chose not to raise my sisters or me. She only raised her boys. Nevertheless, I didn't love her any less. As for my father, there were always rumors of his identity. People whispered in the small town. As I got older, I asked questions, trying to find out who he was, but never got answers. I would be told by my elders, "You don't need to know that." So my entire life, I wondered, who was this man? Did I look like him? Did I act like him? Who was the man responsible for giving me life?

At first, I was just a curious kid, but as I got older, it got more serious. I wanted to know my history, my DNA. As an adult, I endured several illnesses that weren't found on my mother's side of the family—illnesses that probably came from my paternal DNA. From gallstones to cancer, I've had multiple surgeries in my life. Imagine filling out those intense medical forms where they ask you a zillion questions regarding your family medical history and you don't have the answers. Very frustrating. As my mother got older, I would try to get her to reveal my father's identity, but she never did. So I stopped pressing her.

By the time I moved to Chicago in 1968, my mother had married a wonderful man and they became an example of what a successful marriage should look like. He was a deacon in the church, Deacon Charlie Berry.

There was no money for me to attend college, so I worked. Although I was legally an adult when I went to live with my parents,

I still had to abide by their house rules. I had a 2 a.m. curfew. I wanted my freedom. So at the age of 21, I got married because I wanted to live my life and not be constrained by the rules of my mother's house or by the ghosts of Mississippi. My mother warned me that I should wait, live life, and get my own place before I settled down. Just like kids today, I didn't listen because I thought I knew everything. I was in love with my high school sweetheart and wedding bells were on my mind. Actually, freedom was on my mind, but it came with a cost.

Six years later, at the age of 27, I had my daughter, Tenisha Taylor. My husband and I divorced in 1980. Two years later, my ex-husband was killed, and I was left to raise Tenisha all by myself.

During the marriage, my husband was often abusive, but to this day, I never discuss the negative details of my marriage with Tenisha. She has no idea of the trials or tribulations I faced with him. After his untimely death, I decided not to divulge any negative details of our marriage because I wanted Tenisha to remember him the way she wanted to. I didn't want to taint her judgment of the man she called Daddy.

After my first marriage ended, I decided to put all of my energy into raising my daughter. I was a single mother juggling responsibilities and heartaches on my own. I put myself through school. I learned to "rob Peter to pay Paul." I learned to stick up for myself, run a household, balance the books, change tires, fix water heaters, cut grass, shovel Chicago snow, and more! I've been unemployed, underemployed, and self-employed, and sometimes I worked two jobs at once. But through it all, I never lost sight of my goals and my purpose in life. I've been so extremely blessed because my good days have definitely outweighed my bad days. When times got bad I knew that through my deep faith in God I would find my way through.

So I poured all my energy into making Tenisha the woman she is today. Whatever she wanted, I provided. Tap class, ballet class, drama class, flute lessons, guitar lessons, private school, public school… whatever it took to make her well-rounded and successful, I did it. I was single for 18 years. It wasn't easy. I've had no credit, bad credit, bounced checks, and more. There were many nights when I lay in bed wondering what the next day would bring. As always, God brought us through.

When Tenisha went off to college, I was alone. In fact, when the family dropped her off at Clark Atlanta University, I cried all the way home in the car. By hour 10 of me sniffling, my sister finally said, "Would you shut up?!" When we got home, I called Tenisha and she was having the time of her life. I thought to myself, *I better get a life.* I was lonely at first, but not for long.

It happened one night when I was sitting at home preparing for a speech that I had to deliver at church. My phone rang and on the other end was a man who would later become my second husband: Sammie Pate, whom I've known since the second grade. Yes, all the way back in rural Mississippi. He used to pull my ponytails when I was in the second and third grades. In eighth grade, Sammie moved away from Lexington, and we lost contact.

So here was a man on the line who I hadn't heard from in decades. At the time Sammie was grieving, because his wife had recently died from cancer. We began to talk more frequently over the weeks. I explained to him that I was not in a relationship and I didn't want be in a relationship because I had decided to spend my life being committed to the Lord. I was clear with him: I wasn't gonna be cheating on my Lord.

But Sammie said, "I'm looking for a wife. I need a wife."

I think that was around Valentine's Day 1999. We got married on New Year's Day, 2000. Now, that was Y2K. Everybody kept telling me, "You're crazy! You're having a wedding on New Year's Day, Y2K? The world is going to end!" People were predicting all kinds of catastrophes. They were packing and storing food and planning for their afterlife. It didn't even faze me. Because of the walk I had been through with the Lord, I just trusted that everything was going to be all right. I trusted that God had led me to this man, and I knew that nothing would happen to us on January 1, 2000. I've been married to him for 12 years.

I would suggest to every couple getting married now that they have a third string. By that, I mean a relationship with God. Couples need to get some counseling and figure out each of their individual weaknesses and how they can be strong together.

When people ask me my tips for staying married, I always tell them that communication is the number one key. If there's something bothering you, you need to bring it to the table. You need to sit down to discuss it. And if it seems like it's not going to be a good time, then maybe you need to wait. Timing can be critical, so it's important to know your mate well enough to know when and where you should begin any given conversation. Don't let it go too long though, because that can make things get more out of hand.

You should never go to bed mad at each other. You should never leave home without saying "I love you," or if you're too mad to say that, at least give a hug or a kiss. That will make you feel better. Bottom line: If you get mad, you have to make up.

It's important that you communicate and define your roles as husband and wife early on. Decide who's going to wash the dishes, who's going to cook, and so on. Finance is the number two key. A lot of fights will come from having different financial goals. Finances can really ruin a marriage, or any relationship for that matter. As a married couple, you have to talk intimately about finances. Discuss your goals, your credit scores, your spending habits, retirement, and financial fears. You can't have secrets from each other. You can't be out spending money if the other person is saving. One cannot be on one page, and the other person on another page. You've got to be able to talk about what you're going to do. What's the financial plan? Make a plan and stick to it.

I've been a guest at plenty of weddings in my lifetime. Beautiful, elaborate weddings; church weddings, destination weddings. I have seen some serious cash dropped. It's okay to have a big wedding, but I would advise against it. Something more fruitful can be done with the $5,000 that goes towards flowers. A fantastic wedding can cost less than $10,000, so why go in debt to spend $50,000? Buy a house instead, get some property, get something that can bring some extra money.

My husband and I have had two arguments in our 12 years of marriage. We were both set in our ways about doing what we wanted to do, when we wanted to do it. He was a saver, I was a spender. I didn't care if my credit was jacked up; I wanted what I wanted no matter what. I didn't save for a rainy day. So we had to learn the importance of communicating and sharing budgets early on to keep our relationship and our finances healthy.

One thing I do know is that you cannot change a person once you get married. As Mary J. Blige says, "Take me as I am." You have to be comfortable with your partner, accept all of his or her flaws and shortcomings, and realize you cannot turn him or her into the man or woman you want. You're never going to know a person all the way. My advice to young couples now is to try to learn a lot about the other person *before* you start a relationship. Pick up on habits, behaviors, and trends. Follow your gut, and of course, ask God for wisdom and clarity.

When we got married, my husband sensed that there was a part of me missing. I wanted to know who my father was. I wanted to know my medical history, especially during my bout with colon cancer. I started poking around online and asking my siblings if they had any information about my father's identity. My daughter even tried to help me find him. After I suffered through months of frustration, my husband told me to let it rest. He told me when it was time for it to be revealed, then it would be revealed. Boy, was he right! Years later, I finally tracked down my birth father by accident. Well, not an accident… God works in mysterious ways.

My husband worked with a gentleman who casually mentioned to him that he was would soon be having some family in town that hailed from Lexington. My husband replied, "Hey man, my wife and I are from Lexington!" Since it was such a small town, the two figured they probably knew some of the same families. "What's your family's name?" my husband asked the young gentleman.

After days of conversations, phone calls, and questions, I later learned that the man my husband worked with is my nephew. Yes! His dad is my brother. What are the odds that after all those years, and so many miles from Mississippi, a stranger would turn out to be my nephew? Who would have thought in a city as big as Chicago that these two men would work together? My nephew put me touch with my other siblings and also filled me in on the father I never met. Months later, he was transferred to a different location, and my husband never worked with him again. I am convinced that God placed those two men together for a reason. I am now steadfast in praying for divine intervention and divine relationships. God places people in your life for reasons and seasons.

Now, in 2012, I'm entering retirement and reflecting on my life. I look back on the poverty, my rural upbringing, the harsh conditions on the farm, the racism, my strict grandparents, my dumb mistakes, my failed health, my failed relationships, my marriages, my divorce, my jobs, my job losses, the deaths of those close to me, and more. It's an understatement to say that I've had my ups and downs, but one thing is for sure: God has brought me a mighty long way.

My mother, Christine Berry, has now gone home to be with the Lord, but I thank God for allowing me the opportunity to get to spend quality time with her as an adult. Being able to forgive and start fresh in relationships is so important. I now have a wonderful husband, a beautiful home, a wonderful daughter, stepchildren, and grandchildren. More importantly, I am at peace about my father. I could have never imagined a life so fulfilling and rich for myself thirty years ago. Now, I travel, and I'm learning new technology. Who would have thought that a 62-year-old retired woman could embrace the iPad, iPod, Skype, Facebook, and Face Time? I can truly say, "It's not where you're from… It's where you're at." #LookingForwardtomyGoldenYears.

—**Velma Pate**

Velma L. Pate is a retired executive administrator for the Chicago Housing Authority (CHA). For 32 years, she has been a member of the New Covenant M.B. Church, during which time she has served as the president of Mission II Ministry, which is responsible for outreach to less fortunate people in the community. A resident of Glenwood, Illinois, Pate and her husband Sammie have five children and eight grandchildren.

CHAPTER 16

A Love that Is Slow and Steady

MY FIRST RECOGNITION OF LOVE WAS THAT IT WAS something that is tough, solid, and unbreakable, like steel. I learned that from my mother, who was the first love of my life. Looking for a mate, I've always sought women with whom I could enjoy the kind of "durable" love that my mom taught me was important. My mother taught me early on that while the romantic notions of love are important, it is equally special to find a partner who is an asset to my life in every way. She taught me that my spouse should be someone who could make me stronger than I am on my own. I needed someone who could help push life forward, someone who could shield me (and vice versa) from the ups and downs of life. I define love in many parts. There is certainly the physical part of it, but equally important to me is the spiritual aspect.

My high school sweetheart was my first experience with being in love. She was an honest, earnest girl with a good soul who reminded me of my mother. I learned a lot from her, and we dated until I left home for college.

I became very focused on my career after college, but when I was 27, I got married. As foolish as this sounds, part of my motivation was that my mother married and had me at 27, and if she was ready at that age, then I should be as well.

The woman I married was actually a good friend. We were together for 10 years before our relationship ended. That experience taught me that there are a lot of components to a strong marriage, and friendship alone is not enough to make it work. Fortunately, my ex-spouse and I have remained friends and raised our lovely daughters together.

There is a special power in first marriages. My parents divorced when I was 12, but I sometimes romanticize what might have been. Although I know that had my parents stayed together, they would have killed each other, there is still a part of me who sees real beauty in getting it right the first time. I wish, for my sake as well as my ex-wife's and our children's, that we could have gotten it right the first time. I am, however, grateful and humbled that I was able to get it right the second time. My first marriage was a reflection of not knowing myself well enough. You have to know yourself before you can recognize what you need and what you don't need in a mate.

I got it right this time. My wife, Lyne, represents all the things about love that I recognized and felt as a child. Certainly, there is a physical component, and my wife is an extremely beautiful woman— more beautiful now than when we met. Like my mother, she is tough and helps us balance the good times and bad. In life, there are bad times when you need steel to hold things together, but you need steel for the good times as well, because it helps remind you what is real. My wife is very capable of communicating her feelings: what pleases her and displeases her, how she sees me, what her goals are, and what our goals should be. We have a partnership on every level.

I respect my wife tremendously. It is her voice that I hear more than anyone else's when I have to make a career or a personal deci- sion. In my career as an international journalist, I didn't often make time for relationships. It wasn't until I met Lyne, and saw how much she deserved to be loved, that I made real time for love in my life.

I think the way most people live their lives today contradicts what it means to be in love. People have a tendency to be self-centered, and they want to receive love but not give it. Life is complicated, and in the course of any given day there is a lot that we have to deal with that consumes our time and energy. Most people spend their lives in front of a fire hose, and with so much to deal with, they may have trouble recognizing and embracing love. What I've learned is that love is slow and steady, and I think society needs to slow down a little bit. My wife and I have purposefully slowed down. We have simple meals, and we may do one activity a day instead of nine. This has made our connection to one another better and stronger.

My career has taken me into war-torn areas around the world, and when I've covered tragedies and interviewed the survivors, what they often talk about is the last conversation they had with a loved one. Because of these experiences, I have become more sensitive about expressing my feelings for the people who are most important in my life. I now tell my wife each day how much I love her. I know that sounds like a small thing, but she should know that I love her and that she is the most important person in my life. It's important that she completely understands, through both my words and my actions, that she is loved.

—Byron Pitts

Byron Pitts is a correspondent for 60 Minutes *and chief national correspondent for* The CBS Evening News with Scott Pelley.

CHAPTER 17

How My Parents Found Love

IN 1975, MY DAD WAS 27 AND SPENDING THE FIRST OF THREE YEARS in the Peace Corps stationed in the former Republic of Zaire (now called the Democratic Republic of the Congo) in central Africa. He was working with farmers in a rural village to build and manage fishponds, which ensured the farmers both a steady income as well as nutritious food for themselves, their families, and their community.

One day as he was traveling back to his village, he passed a truck that had broken down on the road. On that truck was my mother. She was born and raised in Kikwit, a city now infamous for its 1995 Ebola virus outbreak.

She was 19 and on her way to her village for traditional treatments by her grandmother, which according her family's customs were to ensure a good marriage and healthy children with the man she would soon marry (this arrangement had been promised without her consent from the time she was twelve). Well, fate intervened, and my father, who was immediately smitten, offered to take everyone home on his way back to his village, a three-hour drive. Seizing the opportunity, he asked my mom to sit with him in the truck's cabin while everyone else climbed in the back of the truck. He then suggested that she go with him to his village. The rest, as they say, is history.

Of course, after a few days my mom's grandmother, aunt, and cousin came to take her back home, but she didn't want to leave, and my father didn't want her to go either. Before she left, my mom made my dad promise that he would come get her, and four days later, that's exactly what he did. After meeting with my mother's family and the chief of her clan to negotiate the dowry, they were married. Though they only knew another a few days before marrying, they have now been married 36 years. They have three children: me and my younger sister and brother. We were all born in Africa, but my mother wanted us to receive a US education. So in 1983, when I was five, we moved to the United States.

Moving presented a lot of challenges for my mother. As an immigrant, she didn't speak the language or understand the culture, and she couldn't drive. It took her a long time, but she eventually adapted to her new surroundings. She learned English, got a driver's license, and eventually received her US citizenship. She got a job and put my dad through grad school. Together, they raised my siblings and me, and now we are all doing well as lawyers.

My parents come from completely different backgrounds, races, languages, and cultures; for all intent and purposes, they come from different worlds. Despite this, they built a successful relationship that has withstood the test of time. The foundation of what I am now creating with my husband is rooted in the values I learned from my parents. Like them, my husband and I are committed to overcoming all obstacles that life presents and to making a lasting relationship.

When I look at relationships today, I am disappointed by the lack of commitment people have toward making marriage work. Our society is so committed to freedom of choice that it allows people to choose to leave a marriage for any reason. My parents provided a different example. They showed me that even in the face of adversity, if you are committed to your spouse, you have to do whatever it takes to overcome those challenges and make the marriage work. Because of my parents, I knew that I would forge the same type of bond with the man I chose to marry.

Fortunately, my husband has values, morals, character, dreams, and ambitions that are very similar to my own. Even though we both have a lot to learn, and we are in the early years of our marriage, we are committed to making our relationship top priority and devoting the time and effort to build a lasting foundation for our marriage and family. We learned this from our parents.

—**Marilee Holmes**

Marilee Fiebig Holmes is an immigration attorney in Atlanta. Her practice concentrates on business immigration, including temporary working status and permanent residence for professionals, international transfers, investors, researchers, artists, and athletes. Holmes is married to T.J. Holmes, a journalist.

CHAPTER 18

Finding My Purpose, Finding My Mate

T HE FIRST EXAMPLE THAT I HAD OF A LOVING RELATIONSHIP came from my mother and father. Unlike many of my friends and relatives, I was raised in a two-parent household. I was fortunate to witness firsthand a couple who fought to keep their family together. What I remember most from my childhood is that my parents were willing to invest in my welfare and the welfare of their relationship. While there was romantic love between them, what I remember most is their deep commitment to provide love to their children.

My parents worked constantly to provide my sister and me with a portrait of what it means to be a family unit. I learned how to share love openly, and I also learned that love is not a finite or limited resource. Love is something where the more you give, the more you get.

Growing up, I automatically assumed that I would have a partner. I always thought that I would have a wife. But as I got older, I began to question if that was a reasonable expectation or even a necessary one. I know a number of people who are unmarried but in good relationships, or who have been single for a long time. They are all very happy. Though I am married today, I still do not necessarily think everyone needs to get married. We often hear marriage thrown around as a solution to black woes, but it is not. Healthy relationships of any type are what will help the black community.

In college, I began to wonder how important marriage had to be in my life. I knew that I wanted to be in a space where I could express love and have love expressed to me, but I also knew that marriage came with a lot of distinct challenges. The idea that you would love someone and live with him or her for the rest of your life was daunting. How do you make the decision to be with some-one for the rest of your life when you've only known each other for a few years?

After entering adulthood, I knew that being intimate with a woman significantly increased the chances that I would end up in a long-term partnership with her. So I had to explore where I wanted to spend my time and ask myself, "Who do I want to be with, and does my life purpose allow for a partner?" I have a strong feeling that everyone comes to this planet with a purpose, which, though differ-ent for every individual, is for the collective good.

As I look at black male leadership, I see towering, impressive figures. However, reading about the relationship between Martin and Coretta, or Malcolm and Betty, or even between Barack and Michelle, I have learned that they have all faced challenges. Often, when one person's calling is to be a servant to the community, their partner ends up forsaken. Michelle Obama has remarked that she sometimes felt like being with Barack was like being a single mother and raising their children alone.

I didn't want to be in a relationship that made my partner or me feel single.

Before I was ready to commit to be someone's life partner, I wanted to get a better sense of what I was called to do. I didn't want to automatically assume that I should have a partner, because I believe that my partner's dreams have to at least be complementary to mine. In looking for a life partner, I needed our ideas, goals, and purposes to be in sync. I didn't want to be the person who spent a great deal of time working on his career and purpose only to neglect his partner. Sadly, I have seen the neglecting of partners much more than I've seen healthy relationships within the black community. I didn't want that pattern to continue with me.

Today, black men who are achieving academic success and acquiring wealth know that they are desirable, and too often they treat that fact like it offers them *carte blanche*. They know that when it comes to dating the numbers are on their side. These days, men have been generally socialized to "sow their wild oats"—to go out, experiment, and live their lives freely. When you instill that mentality upon the already limited number of eligible men (men who are educated, employed, etc.), you have a recipe that is potentially damning for black marriages.

It's kind of like when you're young and want to have fun and eat candy, soda, and chocolate. It's enjoyable for a moment, but then it becomes very unfulfilling. In fact, it makes you downright sick. Unfortunately, too many brothers have not yet realized they're not only hurting their potential partners, but also themselves. The more I've grown and watched my friends grow, the more I realize that the enjoyment of "playing the field" is temporary. If you are not seeking relationships that have meaning or that offer support for you to grow, something has to change. That change is something that's often internal, and it can't be taught, mandated, or coerced. It's part of the maturation process into healthy adulthood.

It's very difficult to make a relationship successful. I believe that if I (a sociologist and a black man) am to going commit to enriching the lives of black people, I should be living a life that is a healthy and uplifting example. Once I realized that many of the casual relationships that my peers and I had with women were not healthy for ourselves individually, nor for the community collectively, I decided to get myself ready for the task.

As soon as I figured out that my purpose would allow me to have a mate, and that we could be complementary in our walk in life, I thought, "Let's see who is out there." Now, I didn't grab a checklist with the 15 criteria that I needed, but it was the start of me taking commitment seriously and looking for a life partner. Of course, finding an appropriate partner and building a healthy relationship is difficult and takes work. Ultimately, relationships are works in progress because you never perfect them. Instead, you adapt and evolve to survive and thrive. When I finally felt committed and able to engage in that work of building a relationship, I did it. When I felt committed and able to bring enough to the table where I was clear on who I was, I brought it. When I had the ability to see partners and their potential and really identify them for who they were and not who I perceived them to be, that was when I knew I was ready to find someone who I could walk through this life with and build something greater.

—Dr. R. L'Heureux Lewis-McCoy

Dr. R. L'Heureux Lewis-McCoy is an assistant professor of sociology and black studies at the City College of New York–CUNY. He specializes in racial and ethnic relations, and engages in research and activism that concentrate on educational inequality, race-related public policy, and gender equity.

CHAPTER 19

Love Worth the Wait

I MET MY HUSBAND, EMERY, 35 YEARS AGO WHEN I WALKED INTO the band room of our high school after transferring mid-term. The band was playing, and he was standing on the podium directing. To this day, he says that it was love at first sight, but I really didn't notice him. He was the band captain and drum major that year, extremely smart and, in my opinion, a geek, so of course we were just friends. It was Emery's senior year, and I had two more to go. We kept in touch as he went to Georgia Tech and got a job at IBM. Soon I was at Berry College and enjoying my first taste of freedom.

Life marched on, and after I finished school and began my career in radio, Emery and I kept in touch here and there. I got married and had two boys and soon found out my husband was a crack addict. I was on the rollercoaster from hell. The lies, stealing, manipulations, and the tears—it seemed never-ending. After three long years of moving toward divorce, it was over! I never felt such pain and loss in my life, and my young boys didn't understand why Daddy wasn't living with us.

Emery came back into my life as my friend, stepping in to help me with my boys, taking them to their baseball games, the park, and so on. I could see Emery would be a wonderful father, but he simply was not ready to be my husband, and I told him so. I needed someone to support me in my career and not smother me. He was hurt, but he understood my reservations. Soon after, he married someone else and our lives went in separate directions.

We talked once in a blue moon, and I saw him after about 15 years and we talked about our lives. We were both living the dream with our children; he had two girls, and we both had busy careers, houses, and animals. Life was great! Right? Wrong!

Fast-forward to 2010, my boys were 20 and 22 and going about their lives. My youngest was in the Army, and my oldest was pursuing a career as an organic farmer. I was dating and enjoying the single life, not really looking but hoping someone would want to really get to know the real me and not the broadcaster.

In the meantime, Emery's life was falling apart. His wife had moved away with his girls to another country, and his marriage was over. He was distraught and didn't know where to turn. We were Facebook friends, and one day he commented on one of my positive posts. I asked him how he was doing. I left my number in his inbox to call me so we could catch up.

I soon became his prayer partner, confidante, and counselor. He was a mess, and I made him look at his responsibility for the demise of his marriage. I also told him that he had to go through the process—he couldn't skip any of it. It was tough seeing my friend go through so much pain, but it was necessary. I could certainly relate as I had gone though it just as hard: separation, divorce, and not seeing your children is tough, no matter who is to blame.

Slowly, he began to heal, to smile and laugh again. That happy spirit that I knew long ago was emerging again. He was hanging out with my family, and they all remembered him from years ago. He was welcomed with open arms. He and my eldest son in particular spent a tremendous amount of time together. It was good male bonding, and Emery was teaching him things that he would need in the world, things I couldn't possibly teach him as a woman. It was a beautiful thing to see!

I was still dating and trying to think of which of my girlfriends would be a good match for him. He was such a gentleman, and he deserved someone to love him. He liked going out and doing things instead of vegging out on the couch. He wasn't even a sports fanatic—I thought, *What a great catch for somebody!* He let me know that he wasn't interested in anyone else except me, so the answer was no for any blind dates, fix-ups, or anything like that. I never thought we could be in a relationship. I just didn't think we would be compatible; he was still that endearing geek from school in my mind. And besides that, he needed time to heal from his 17-year-long, chaotic marriage.

Well, for my birthday, my wonderful son bought me an external drive for my computer and tried to move my treasured, copyrighted nature photos onto it. *Poof,* they disappeared! After I finished losing it, I called Emery, told him the story, and asked if he could retrieve them. He said he thought he could, so he came over and began to break my computer down and rebuild it. He added memory and programs that I've always wanted but couldn't afford, and the final product was an almost-new computer with my pictures safe and sound. Ha—I told you he was a geek! It took him almost three weeks to complete the job, and during that time I was going out on dates and events. When I would get home, sometimes he'd be there still working, or asleep in the chair. I'd wake him up so we could talk and laugh about the evening's happenings. We became really close friends. It felt natural, just like the old days!

We made it through the holidays and the New Year together as great friends hanging out and going to parties. Sometime in the middle of 2011, I was praying one night. God said to me that Emery was my husband, and I said, oh no, he's like my best friend, I don't want to ruin that. I had not even thought of him in that way at all. But then I thought of all the characteristics I desired in a husband: affection, support, wit, understanding, generosity, kindness, love, and most of all, a man after God's heart. Well, I'll be—Emery had all of that and more!

He professed his love for me as he had done for months and all of a sudden, my heart opened up. We began our courtship and continued to deepen our friendship day by day—I wanted to make sure he had unloaded that suitcase full of 17 years' worth of drama he had been carrying. When he asked me to marry him, I said yes. I've learned that we must look beyond the outward appearance and look at the heart! We must really see the other person through God's eyes—Wow! Just beautiful!

I've since replaced the word *geek* with *techie*. I believe that God was preparing him for me just as I was being prepared for him. God knows our hearts and He gives us our desires. God crafted the perfect husband for me at this time in my life, when I really believe I would never get married again, but He knew my heart. Our friends all say,

"He finally got you after all these years!" Yes, he did, and it's certainly been worth the wait!

—**Twanda Black**

Twanda Black is the public affairs director as well as a talk show and gospel host for KISS 104.1 FM in Atlanta. She is the mother of two young adult sons, and her youngest is currently serving in Afghanistan. Black is an ordained minister, an amateur photographer, a writer, and newly wed to Emery!

CHAPTER 20

The Alpha Woman...Take the Gloves Off at Home, Honey!

I GREW UP ON THE SOUTH SIDE OF CHICAGO IN THE LATE '70S AND early '80s. Unfortunately, at a very young age, I experienced the death of a parent. Beyond the grief of the sudden tragedy, what I didn't know is that my father's death would be the reason why I am the woman I am today...an alpha woman.

I recall the evening of his death ever so vividly. We had a green phone stationed on our kitchen wall. You remember back in the day, when there was only one phone in the house? It was centrally located so that everyone could use it. No, not a cordless phone or a cell phone. Those weren't out then...or if they were, they didn't figure into my parents' budget. I'm talking about the phone in a common area of the house where everyone could hear your conversation. If you wanted to talk to your friends, you had to stand propped in that one position until the conversation was over. I remember that we eventually got a long curly cord to help us maneuver through the house while chatting, but when that cord got tangled, it took divine intervention to unravel it. Nevertheless, it was our lifeline. There was no Facebook, no Twitter, no Tango, no Skype, no Face Time, no texting...just that ugly, green phone.

One night as my mom and I were sleeping in her bed, that green phone rang. My mom, startled awake, walked toward the kitchen to answer. On the other end was terrible news—news about my father that would forever change our lives. I peeked through the bedroom door and had a straight line of sight to my mom leaning against the kitchen wall holding that green phone. She projected a look of despair, disgust, pain, and horror.

Just as her sister-in-law was telling her about my father's death, there came several panicked knocks at the door. More like banging. Loud banging. To my tender ears, it sounded like thunderous pounding, the scariest sound I had ever heard in my life. My mom dropped that green phone and ran to our front door. On the other side, Chicago police. "Ma'am, are you Velma Taylor?" my mom replied, "Yes, sir, I am." He went on, "Ma'am, is your husband Ezekiel Taylor?" to which she answered, "Yes, sir, he is." And then came the dreaded news that no wife ever wants to hear: "Mrs. Taylor, I'm sorry to tell you, but we've just found your husband dead." Right then, at that very moment, two alpha women were born…my mom and me.

I had to watch my mother, at the young age of 31, make funeral arrangements and plans to bury her husband. She became the secretary, the researcher, the primary caregiver, the decision maker, the CEO, and the CFO of our family all in the matter of just one week. She ran an organized, tight ship as she prepared to say goodbye to her high school sweetheart. There was no time for emotion. She had paperwork to complete, phone calls to make… the crying would have to come later. That week, my mother took charge, and she stayed strong and in charge for the rest of my childhood.

As a result of my father's death, I grew up in a single-parent household. No, let me rephrase that—I grew up with a single alpha mother. She said what she meant, and she meant what she said. She never asked for handouts, she never begged, and she never lived on public assistance. My father's untimely death thrust her into the workforce. Before his death, she was a high school graduate with no college experience. She was a part-time worker whose main job was really to take care of her daughter…me. Her role shifted, and she became responsible for the mortgage, the bills, and the food on the table. And what about the grass that needed cutting, or the snow that needed shoveling? She did it. She became a woman forced to take on the role of her late husband.

Over the years, I watched my mother do everything. And I mean *everything*! She was in charge. She fixed her car, she hand-washed her car, she fixed the toilet when it was stopped up, and she even once tried to drag in a hot water heater when ours broke. I never saw her ask a man for help. In fact, she *was* the man, as comedian Steve Harvey explains in his book, *Act Like a Lady, Think Like a Man*. Harvey says women like my mom are so used to doing everything on their own that they become their own man. Sure, on occasion, my mom would have to call a plumber, a mechanic, or an electrician, but that was the extent of her asking for a man's help. She got up for work every day and got me dressed for private school. She made her own money and paid her own bills. The thought of relying on a man to take care of her probably never entered her mind. She never dated when I was young. It was just the two of us.

As many scholars believe, people are a product of their environment. And after looking back over my life, I must agree. Growing up, I developed into a type A assertive woman. I was very aggressive and vocal in high school. Usually, I was the leader of the group. I was an honor student, president of the Honor Society, and captain of the cheerleading team. I was never bullied, and as an only child, I had no problems sticking up for myself. Hmm, I wonder where that came from?

I guess you could say my mom and I were like two peas in a pod. I was witness to her assertiveness when she received bad customer service. I was there when a bill collector tried to bully her. I can recall every time she stood up for herself and me. She was a lioness! She could be sweet and soft, but don't try to mess over her, her house, or her cub. She would cut like a knife! She never accepted no for an answer. She taught me how to go out and get whatever I wanted in life, and most importantly she taught me how to earn my own money at an early age and depend on no one.

The summer before my freshman year of high school, I wanted my own money, but I wasn't of legal working age. That didn't stop me—at the age of 13, I became a cashier for a local wing and hamburger joint. I got paid $90 a week to work Monday through Friday, noon until 5 p.m., and I got paid under the table. Yes, $90 tax-free a week. That was a lot of money for a 13-year-old. But I was responsible. I took public transportation to work. I greeted my customers with a smile and pleasantly handed them their food and change.

Then, at the age of 16, I remember telling my mother that I wanted to be a journalist. My mom had a friend who was close friends with the publisher of the *Chicago Citizen* newspaper. She got his number and politely called the gentleman, whom she had never met.

"Mr. Garth, my name is Velma Taylor and I am a friend of Joe Ewing. He told me to give you a call." Not giving him a chance to put her on hold, she quickly went on. "You see, my daughter wants to be a journalist and I was wondering if she could come spend some time in your office at the *Citizen* newspaper?"

Mr. Garth didn't hesitate. "Sure, I'll let her spend some time with our managing editor, Ms. Lisa Ely."

I reflect on that scenario and think, "Gosh, my mom had balls!" To call a newspaper publisher during his busy work hours to ask if her daughter could visit really took some guts. She probably would have barged into Mayor Daley's office if I had wanted to be a politician. Whew, that's an alpha woman for you.

I showed up at my first day dressed like a mini-professional. I shadowed Lisa around the office, in awe of her command and her professionalism. By the next summer, I was working at the *Citizen* newspaper as a typesetter, and by my senior year, I was writing articles. I followed Lisa everywhere she went. She even went to the black newspaper convention in Minneapolis, and Mr. Garth paid for me to go with her. Being in Lisa's presence helped define who I wanted to be. She was an intelligent, assertive, yet still Christian woman of Delta Sigma Theta Sorority, Inc. She was another alpha woman. By the end of that summer, I was also evolving into an alpha woman.

For college, I wanted to be on my own. As close as my mother and I were, I wanted to show her that, I, too, could stand on my own. With a full scholarship from Mr. Garth's Quentis Bernard Garth (QBG) Foundation, I was able to attend Clark Atlanta University. My mom, grandmother, aunts, and cousins packed me up and drove me the 800-plus miles to Atlanta, Georgia. They stayed my entire first week, and when they left, I witnessed my mother crying for the very first time. In fact, I can't recall another time even now. I know she has lived through pain, she lived through not knowing how the bills would get paid, she lived through loneliness, but not once did I see her cry. But at this moment, at this time, a mother's joy and pride for her daughter bled out of her heart for all to see.

While a student at Clark Atlanta, my interest in becoming a newspaper reporter turned into a desire to become a television reporter. But after one semester of reporting and anchoring, one of my professors noticed my alpha woman demeanor. I recall one professor, Reggie Mitchell, saying to me, "Tenisha, you know you really ought to think about producing instead of reporting."

"What's that?" I asked.

He replied, "You would be in charge of putting the newscast together."

I wondered why he thought I would be good at that, and he had no problem answering me: "Because you're always trying to be in charge… just so bossy!" Professor Mitchell, like my mom and Lisa, helped solidify my alpha woman character.

From there, I spent the next several years as a television news producer in a variety of cities. It's a dog-eat-dog industry, where only the strongest survive. It's very competitive, and often, there is back-stabbing. There's a lot of cursing and yelling and high tension in this field.

Then in 2003, the call from CNN came. I flew from DC down to Atlanta and accepted a job as a news producer, and two years later I was promoted to executive producer. This promotion didn't go over well with everyone, and there was a lot of criticism and whispering: "Who is this woman?" "Where did she come from?" "How old is she?" "What's her background?" I had to stand tall and meet all adversaries head-on, with class and professionalism. I overcame several obstacles and an episode or two of sabotage, but I survived.

As an executive producer on a national level, I have to be an alpha woman. It is almost mandatory in order to survive. I have to know how to manage a team of people who all have different personalities and needs. I have to make quick decisions and be knowledgeable about current events. I have to convince people twice my age why I deserve to be their boss. I must always mind my p's and q's and know when to say no and when to say yes. I have to know when someone is truthful and know when someone is dicking me around.

I've had a lot of challenges and I've learned a lot of important lessons as an executive producer. I've lasted for almost 10 years at CNN, probably thanks to my aggressive alpha woman attitude. My career, however, hasn't turned out to be my biggest challenge.

In 2010, I was fortunate enough to marry my best friend. He too, is a member of the media, a television reporter. And he is an alpha male! He is my biggest challenge. Mr. Craig Bell is what you would call a "man's man." He stands 6-foot-2 and tips the scale at almost 300 pounds. He's a former college running back and has no problems running over whoever or whatever gets in his way. He is an authoritative, assertive, type A, deep-baritone-speaking man. He stands up for what he believes in, challenges authorities when they are wrong, and fights for the little people. These are all qualities that attracted me to him, but never did I realize that for us to cohabit in the same house, someone would have to back down.

And he made it clear that it wasn't going to be him. Craig was the *man* of the house, and I needed to simmer down. The woman I was at work was not the woman he needed at home. It's like I had to learn to be two different people.

Craig is very traditional. The man is the head of the house, the man does the heavy lifting, and the man takes care of his wife, his children, and his house. First it's God, then man, and then woman. I, however, was used to being the man. I did everything in my house, just like my mom did in hers. I never asked a man for help. And growing up, I never saw what a "wife" was supposed to be. What was this "wife" role? I had no idea.

During our courting season, we realized that these two alpha personalities would soon kill each other. So we enrolled in premarital classes at our church to help us understand our roles. We (especially me) had to learn to stay in our lanes, or there would be a severe collision on the road. Our pastor had to explain a few things to us.

He told Craig, "She's been in charge all her life, she's in charge at home and at work, she is running all of the time looking out for her, so she just doesn't know how to stop and take the gloves off."

To me, he said, "Craig is a man's man. You must submit some of your authority. Take the gloves off and let him be the man. Let down your guard. Don't be so harsh, commanding, or assertive. God has sent you this man to take care of you, so let him. He is your pillar."

Hearing this wasn't easy. In fact, I had to explain to Craig and my pastor that it would have to be a learned behavior. You can't potty train a toddler at the snap of a finger. You can't just stop being a chain smoker in one day, and my alpha woman personality wouldn't change overnight.

When Craig and I moved in together, he didn't understand why I was hell-bent on doing everything myself. I didn't understand why it mattered so much to him. When I didn't ask for his help, he felt that he wasn't needed. I made all kinds of decisions on my own, and when I made them, he felt I was disrespecting him, which I would never do to my husband on purpose.

What Craig didn't realize is that I just didn't know how to be a "wife." It is a learned behavior. There is a reason why the Bible talks about wives being "submissive." There is a reason why marriage vows have the woman repeat "to love and obey." That is the natural order of things. If you follow me down the biblical path, men were in *charge*, bottom line.

Women are the supporters, the helpers, and the encouragers. We aren't supposed to be making all the decisions, cutting the grass, signing the mortgage, shoveling the snow, or changing the tires. God made men to perform those grueling tasks. However, our society now has everything backwards. Where are the men who run their households? Why is it that sources report that around 60 percent of households in the United States are run by single women? Our society is out of order. And I needed to get that through my thick skull if my marriage was going to last. I needed to take off the gloves. In fact, I remember Craig telling me early in our marriage that there would only be "one set of balls in this house."

I remember vividly how once, over the course of several days, the light bulbs in our high-ceiling kitchen blew out, one by one. I was home alone when the final two bulbs blew out and it was dim. Being an alpha woman, I simply grabbed the bulbs from the pantry and started to work. I stood on a chair and then climbed on top of the island counter to change the bulbs. Oh, I failed to mention: I was six months pregnant at the time, and standing on a countertop changing bulbs.

Craig came home to a brightly lit kitchen and asked of his pregnant wife, "Who changed the bulbs?" I said, "I did."

He had a fit! It wasn't that he was upset about his bright kitchen. He was upset that I had once again stepped into his lane. Once again, I performed a job that the man of the house should perform—not to mention while I was pregnant. He was livid that I would risk my safety and the safety of our baby.

Another time, I was home all day and the huge industrial trash bin in our kitchen became full. Instead of just getting another bag, I decided to pull out this humongous bag that was almost twice my size, drag it outside, lift it up, and put it in our trash can. Once again, the alpha male entered the house.

"Hey, babe, who took the trash out?"

Feeling ashamed, like Eve when God came into the Garden of Eden, I humbly answered, "I did."

Once again, Craig was furious with me. He scolded me, saying no woman of his would be taking out the trash. Then he added, "What would the neighbors think?" *Wow*, what if all men thought like this...

While I was feeling like a six-year-old, being reprimanded not to do that again, it got me wondering. What *if* all men felt the same way? What would the neighbors think if a man left his child? What would the neighbors think if he didn't work? What would the neighbors think if he didn't take care of business? What would the neighbors think if his pants were sagging down? We would have a nation of strong men, leaders, husbands, dads, and father figures.

Craig isn't terribly worried about what others think. He's just focused on being a good strong husband, and to do that, he needs a wife who doesn't constantly challenge his manhood or his authority. It's taken me a while to understand this notion. Thankfully, I have women of wisdom in my life who are coaching me to be a better wife. They tell me, "Take the gloves off, honey, you're home."

Some days their advice works…and other days, I'm a rebellious hell-raiser. I know my alpha woman character sometimes makes me come across as a woman who doesn't need a man. But I do. I need his love, compassion, protection, friendship, and wisdom.

I have so many hard-working, independent, successful, home-owning girlfriends who think that they don't need a man, but ladies, *you do.* Trust me, you do. Now I just have to learn how to soften myself at home to let my man take the lead. I don't have to always be in charge, no matter what society taught me as a young girl growing up with my alpha mom. She was an alpha woman because she had to be. She had to make every decision.

The difference with me is that I don't. After being married for a few years now, I realize that I can't compete with Craig's role as the man. In order for my marriage to survive, I must learn how to be two distinctly different women. The alpha woman has to stay at work. I have to "leave my balls in the car" when I come home.

So it seems that I have met my match. I must admit that it has been the biggest challenge of my life so far. Sometimes I do well, and sometimes I fail. But when I see that alpha woman raising her ugly head, I have to remember to put her back in my briefcase. Take the gloves off, honey, you're home.

—**Tenisha Taylor Bell**

Tenisha Taylor Bell is an executive producer at CNN, which is based in Atlanta, Georgia. A graduate of Clark Atlanta University, she is a board member of the YWCA of Greater Atlanta and a member of Delta Sigma Theta Sorority, Inc. Bell lives with her husband, Craig, and their son.

PART III
DIVORCED

That Was Then. This Is Now.

It slipped through my thoughts like shattered glass.
Holes for my soul to slip through.
Particles, specks of me, landed in several directions.
Scattered, but not broken.
That was then.

Shackled to a self-inflicted suffering soul broke my spirit.
Initially I felt empathy, tried to help, offer solutions.
Eventually I learned that I couldn't learn his lessons for him.
He had to do the work himself, and only when he was ready.
Six years seemed an eternity to wait. That was then.
Abram was my slave name.
Now I am free.
Call me Love. This is now.

"I'll be happy when…
    I make more money
    I get a better car
    I get a promotion
    I make more money than you," he said.
But even when what he thought happiness was manifested, it still
wasn't enough.
The notes and chords that constructed his tunes remained brittle
and unharmonious.
He wasn't happy with him
And if he didn't like himself, How could he ever love
Me?
That was then.

Eventually I found the pieces of
Me
That I'd lost underneath an umbrella of failed attempts.
The remnants of my spirit that slipped away,

Unable to breathe under the sodded blanket
Of his displeasure with himself, snuck back into
Me
One day, when the sun and the moon simultaneously
bathed the sky.

I sucked my achievements inside me, knowing
That he internalized my gains as his failure.
Silence.

A brown leaf falls. The only one left on the tree.
The other leaves had turned, bursts of boisterous yellow, ubiquitous
orange, and resilient reds.
Alive. They crowd the brown leaf out, closing their ears to his
broken chords.
The lone leaf sails in the wind, drifting, drifting, reaching the ground.
It stays. This is now.

"Reduce your light so that his can shine," the church counselors said.
Goes against everything I've learned about love, acceptance, and
marriage.
But I concur.
Things get worse. That was then.

I stand in a meadow full of weeping willows
Their branches heavy with blooms. The wind
Steals some away each time it marches through.
The blooms whirl around me, covering me, surrounding me.
Soon there are enough enveloping me. I too am lifted, soaring
through the meadow
Like a kite on a string. Happy. Free. Hopeful.
He pulls the string. Steers me back down to the cold, hard earth
With so much turbulence that I'm dismembered.
I see parts of me floating away on the stem of blooms,
Hiding in the folds of the weeping willows.
That was then. This is now.

I'm a plastic doll. Someone else forms me, changing my
Hair, clothes, words, and actions to suit them. I am thoughtless.
Pulling me off the shelf. Change. Putting me back on the shelf.
Change.
That was then.

Still my heart bled at the end of my beginning in one surly summer.
Standing in the closet we once shared. The earth oil fragrance he
wore still
Stinging the air. Empty hangers in the closet. Cool sheets next to
me at night. Too much room in the bed now. Speaking into the air.
Echoes.
No response.
Brunch. Dinner. A table for one. Brows lifted. Pity oozing.
Staining my pillow with tears. Bleak eyes. Hollow heart.
I learned the posture of being one after six years of being two.
All part of the birthing process.
That was then.

Lack of confidence and self-loathing breeds isolation.
Siamese twins. Bonded by one's needs.
The loner suffocated me. Twills of nonsense. Trepidation.
Do I speak? Should I ask what's wrong? And risk wrath!
Silence. That was then.

Peeking from underneath an unwanted shield, I extend my arms.
Daring to unfold my legs and stretch,
To reach for the pearl orbs of cotton in the azure sea above.
The sun skates across my face,
Its warmth races through my veins. I bow my head in deference.
I can speak. I can feel. I can think. For
Me.
This is now.

—**Trina Love**

Trina Love enjoys verbs and adjectives, a nice cool glass of New Zealand sauvignon blanc, an exciting football game, hanging out at the drive-in, her family (including her dog Romo), and being stretched in every yoga pose imaginable. She's been reading and writing since kindergarten, but developed her writing skills at Georgia State University with a bachelor of arts in advanced writing and rhetoric. Love is currently completing her MFA in professional writing at Savannah College of Art and Design (SCAD). She's been a technical writer and editor for over 18 years, writing technical manuals, online help, and web content for Fortune 500 companies. Love enjoys writing fantasy fiction, and her stories have won numerous writers' contests. Follow Love on Twitter @Yogawriter.

CHAPTER 1

---•---

Where Did Our Love Go?

BLACK RELATIONSHIPS ARE IN TROUBLE. IN FACT, OUR relationship difficulties represents the most pressing issue of our time. That is not debated.

What *is* debated is the source of the intrinsic trouble. Typically, in order to understand a problem, one has only to look at the root of the problem. However, when it comes to the problem of Black Love, there are far too many opinions on how the trouble began. And the answer one may garner from the average black man or black woman will depend on that person's personal history.

I prefer facts. And if we examine historical facts, we will come to understand the ugly truths that brought us to the diminishment of Black Love.

How did we get to this point? We can blame racism, we can blame classism, and certainly, we can point a finger at institutionalized preferential treatment of whites over blacks. However, the real ugly raw answer is that blacks must also share the blame.

We must examine our history. Where we once had thriving communities full of Black Love, we now have communities abandoned by the very people complaining about not being able to find Black Love.

The community and Black Love were first abandoned in the 1970s by the middle- and upper-class blacks who benefited from affirmative action; set-asides; corporate window dressing; and educational benefits won in the '60s as a result of marches, sit-ins, and so on; or from simply being black in a time when that got them so much community support that they could sell almost anything and get votes for almost any office. Blacks ascended corporate ladders and made millions of dollars as professional athletes, musicians, singers, and so on, and almost immediately "loaded up the truck and moved to Beverly…Hills, that is."

Yes, blacks abandoned the community by the droves. White flight from urban areas nearly became a joke, as black families began "moving on up" like the Jeffersons and made every human effort to get away…from low-income blacks.

Communities disintegrated as successful role models emptied out of urban areas across the nation. Factory jobs became a thing of the past as factories largely moved to foreign countries, where labor could be had for cheaper. Even black mom-and-pop businesses left the 'hood while immigrants moved in, employing their own. Low-income blacks left behind had to struggle to make it on fewer job opportunities and dwindling government assistance, and while some made it up and out, others continued to spiral downward.

As the economy worsened in the 1980s, blacks once again became the boogeymen, serving as scapegoats for all of the country's ills. The following fallacies became fodder for political campaigns: "Whites would fare better in the working world if not for affirmative action"; "Whites would have more educational opportunities as well"; "Welfare would not be such a burden on the nation, if not for those welfare-dependent blacks."

The real-life solutions to the fallacious problems? Attacking government assistance in every way possible and moving away from the goal of parity in the workplace. The result: dwindling job opportunities and dwindling government assistance.

Some 'hood denizens ran on the newest fast track for success— the drug game. That brought its own evils, which were even more insidious than racism. It demanded a devaluation of human life and territorial violence. Crack cocaine wreaked havoc on the black community, sending too many black men to jail, too many black women to prostitution, and far too many of both to hell in a dirty gasoline handbasket.

And the privatization of prisons made black men the "product" for the prison industrial complex.

Yes, the 1980s were troubling years for blacks. That decade saw the first wholesale embrace of neoconservatism, which was really classism and racism packaged as "protecting the wealthy." And any Negros who imagined themselves wealthy also imagined that the Republican Party would take care of them, and so they joined, ignoring the racism while trying to focus on personal benefit.

This era was dubbed the Me Decade, because people in the United States were focusing on themselves and disconnecting from the whole. Blacks were not immune to the Me Decade mentality. For the first time in our history in the United States, blacks began to operate as individuals.

The civil rights generation inherited a legacy of overcoming and delivered a legacy of selfishness to the next generation. Two generations earlier, parents slaved away at two blue-collar jobs or went to night school to improve their earning potential and saved, saved, saved...for their children.

The subsequent generation enjoyed better opportunities and increased earning power, and saved, saved, saved...for bigger cars and houses for themselves. This selfishness has manifested itself in relationships where the average person over 30 is seeking someone who is *giving* as opposed to someone with whom they are *sharing*. That's how some black women can justify proclaiming that they want a man "on their level." Where once couples used to always join their two incomes together, black women began to tell each other that whatever they earned was theirs, and that any man they dated would have to match or beat their earnings.

This would not be such a problem if the black community didn't already have so many problems. Seeking someone "on their level" meant that men who were otherwise good and decent were dismissed, further reducing the pool of ostensibly eligible black men. This pool now appears ever smaller to the average black woman caught up in this anti-black-man propaganda.

Yes, at the end of the never-ending assault on black existence, the good old United States turned up the power on the anti-black-man machine. That anti-black-man machine has been unleashing powerful propaganda that has begun to work so perfectly that anyone can say anything about black men and anyone will believe it without question, including black women.

For example, it has become popular for black women to proclaim a "shortage" of black men, due to their love for white women, their failure to flourish financially, and of course, the ever-popular lie about there being more black men in prison than in college.

Many black women have become comfortable with such lies, because they prefer to ignore their own culpability in why they aren't married. The lies are easy scapegoats; they remove all personal responsibility. And now, black men, including this writer, are battling the anti-black-man machine propaganda with truth.

Let's dispel some of the myths used to explain why there aren't enough available black men and why fewer black women are getting married today than in earlier decades. First, according to the latest data from the 2010 US Census, more than 90 percent of all married black men are married to black women. What was that about the black man's alleged love of white women?

As for there not being enough black men "on the level," I want to vomit when I hear this lie. While women have certainly made strides toward parity in the workplace, the reality is that men still outpace women as far as earning power. Black men outpace women in terms of middle management and executive positions. And, according to the US Census Bureau, 68.1 percent of all black men over the age of 16 are in the civilian labor force, compared to 62.3 percent of black women over the age of 16. And even *if* black women were doing so much better than black men, the goal of marriage is partnership. That means if a black woman makes $75,000 per year and her black man "only" makes $60,000 per year, they have a combined financial spending power of $135,000.

Let's next tackle the myth about there being more black men in prison than in college. This misleading statistic comes from such studies as the one conducted by the Justice Policy Institute (JPI), a Washington-based research group. JPI found in 2004 that there were 791,600 black men in jail or in prison, and "only" 603,032 black men enrolled in colleges or universities. They presented the findings as "evidence" that more black men are in prison than in college.

These numbers are misleading, and I believe they were set up to be misleading. In the JPI study, the 791,600 black men found to be in jail or prison includes men of *all ages,* from teenagers to age 94, while black college students are for the most part in their late teens and early twenties. And even then, the numbers are close. If we actually compare age range to age range, there are more black men in college than prison.

Additionally, while there is a higher representative percentage of black men in prison versus the rest of the US male population, the raw number isn't that high.

Any of us can do the math: Out of the roughly 50 million African Americans the 2010 Census measured, less than 1 million are in jail or prison (0.792 million). The reality is that while there are too many of us in prison and more of us in there than other races, there are *not* more of us on the inside than on the outside.

So why does it seem like there are more sisters than brothers on college campuses? Well, there are a number of reasons, which include the evaporation of after-school programs, the dwindling of financial aid programs, and the like. But a huge part of the reason has nothing to do with race. According to the US Department of Education, male undergraduates account for 44 percent of student population, while female undergraduates account for 56 percent. This gender disparity is not race-specific.

What is race-specific, however, is that the traditional programs, such as affirmative action, that bolstered black male college enrollment and the after-school programs designed to keep them occupied and focused were shot to hell in the 1990s. Females are outpacing males across all races. According to the Department of Education, girls get better grades than boys and pursue more strenuous academic programs. The National Center for Education Statistics (NCES) reports that girls outnumber boys in student government, honor societies, and debate clubs. As a writer, I've known for years that girls read more books than boys.

The NCES has also found that boys only excel in sports, school suspensions, dropouts, and diagnoses of ADD (attention deficit disorder). Beyond the classroom, boys outpace girls in crime and substance abuse.

So there are fewer boys than girls in school. Does that translate into fewer available men? Not hardly. The reality is that there aren't fewer good black men or fewer good black women. We are simply having a harder time finding each other.

The fact is that more than ever before, people in the United States are transients and commuters. Many of us work in a world where we don't socialize, and socialize in a world where we don't live, yet we complain about not finding what we want. Communities are fragmented, clubs are polluted with people who have ill intent, and churches mislead people into having relationships with others who attend church service but who do little to follow the teachings of the ministries.

The way we socialize now has diverged from yesteryear, and now women attend seminars, participate in interviews for negative magazine articles, and watch television specials to find out where the men are.

Where are the men? Men have to eat, so they are in grocery stores, where the deli food is fast but far better than fast food. They are at gas stations, because their cars need fuel. And, they are in the local malls, where they purchase clothing, music, and other goods. The men are in the same places as the women—scattered in and out of the community.

In addition to not living or working in the same places, we just don't interact the way we used to. We no longer practice the traditions of yesteryear, when family members would act as match-makers, as well as pass on valuable information about getting along in relationships. Now we live in a world where most of us are making it up as we go along, pretending that we have it all figured out because we've read the relationship book of the month—even if it was written by a thrice-divorced comedian who did no research.

The reality is that there has been a breakdown in society, and men are having the same problems dating as women. It's just not as bad because there are more women than men to begin with. It's bad, but the blame lies with changes in society more than anything else.

I'll say it again, but differently: As a direct result of integration and affirmative action, many of us work in a world where there are few like us, and live on a block where there are also few like us. Yet we complain about not finding us, and talk about the sorry state of those of us we run into.

As black men's numbers decreased on college campuses, our community was splintering, the middle class and above separating themselves from the base of our community. The result is that many educated black women who see themselves as middle class rarely come in contact with black men who also see themselves as middle class. Worse, these men and women no longer live next door to black families of the middle and upper class.

Interaction between post-collegiate black men and women has decreased over time, giving black women the illusion that male black college graduates (or any other single, progressive black men) don't actually exist. And if we buy into the myths and misinformation, things appear worse than they actually are.

Sadly, many of us create myths and misinformation all on our own. Based on my own research, the average person is intimately involved with 15 or fewer people. Out of the roughly 50 million black people in the United States, people are basing their perspectives on only 15 people or less.

Fifty years ago, the Supreme Court's ruling in *Brown v. Board of Education* stated that separating blacks because of their race brought feelings of "inferiority as to their status in the community that may affect their hearts and minds in a way unlikely ever to be undone." The oppression of a people leaves emotional scars that run deep into the self-esteem of the oppressed. These scars grow within the community and perpetuate themselves as efficiently as folk tales, songs, and disease. It can only get worse with other blacks now dogging us out.

We don't need anyone to pontificate on how bad things are, because as bad as the situation is, the badness is overly apparent. What we need now is action and truth. And we need change.

> We ourselves have to lift the levels of our community, the standard of our community to a higher level, make our own society beautiful so that we will be satisfied. We've got to change our minds about each other.
>
> —Malcolm X

Here's the good news: Black people are still getting married. No matter what we hear about how hard it is to find each other, some of us are still finding each other and getting married. If some of us can, others can.

The 2010 Census data reveal that about 30 percent of all black women and about 40 percent of all black men are categorized as married. And we already know that of the black men who are married, more than 90 percent are married to black women.

If the world was a magical place and I could make a wish, I would wish for black men and women to begin to change their minds about each other, as Brother Malcolm longed for. Perception is reality, and we must begin to perceive each other differently so that we can love each other again. If we see ourselves differently, we can see a different future. I know black people can do it.

The diaspora of black people are a special and wonderful blend of horrible oppression, faith, hope, creativity, spirituality, and unresolved issues. No matter how bad things are, collectively we still have what it takes to make it better. Haven't we always?

We can have healthy relationships by seeing each new person as a new person. We can have healthy relationships by keeping other people, and other people's politics, out of our relationships.

We can have healthy relationships by letting go of all the bad things that happened in the past. We can have healthy relationships by placing those bad things in perspective and assigning fault where it really belongs, including partially with us.

We can have healthy relationships by making lists of what we want and what we have to offer that are anchored in reality, so that we can be open to something real, as opposed to something we read about or saw on television, but really don't understand. As Malcolm said, we just have to change our minds and in order to do that, we have to have faith.

Please, keep the faith—faith in yourself and faith in the struggle of life. Faith in the fact that you have to stay in the game, because even if you don't win, at least you are in the game and we all know that's what's real—being in the game, dig me? Keep the faith in your dreams and keep dreaming. Dream of life and dream of love, because right now, everything is possible.

As Malcolm said, we just have to change our minds. Then more of us will be open to Black Love.

Where did our love go? Nowhere. It's been here all along.

—Darryl James

Darryl James is an award-winning author of four books, including the powerful new anthology Notes From the Edge. *James's stage play,* Love in a Day, *opened in Los Angeles in 2011. Reach James at djames@theblackgendergap.com.*

CHAPTER 2

Found Love in a Hopeless Place

THREE YEARS AGO, I WAS A SOUL-SHATTERED, SKITTISH, AND scared new divorcée with crazy therapy bills and an uncomfortable new haircut. I was not my best self. This was when the universe shoved the most unlikely person in front of me, saying, "You two, it's gonna be magic, I see it."

On paper, it was ridiculous. We had massive gaps in background, experience, and, well, age. (Scandalously young is the new black, didn't you know?) My people were puzzled and faux-patient. I could not be serious about this rough-around-the-edges Brooklyn kid. His people were equally baffled. Who's the fancy career lady with the white-girl voice—is she *40*, Son?

You've heard the theory that we all come from soul tribes? And you can instantly spot someone from your tribe? That's how this was. Immediate "me, too!" soul recognition. I see you, I get it all, and I want to bake you into a shrinky-dink and carry you around in my neon lacquered clutch.

That's how it was when we met. I was a top editor at an online magazine and he worked in the mailroom. It was my first week, and I was wearing a clingy little retro Prince tee—my lifelong obsession with him borders on the messianic; there are tattoos involved—and this dangerously cute young guy appears in my doorway carrying, like, 15 bags of makeup.

"Hi. You're Tia Williams?"

"Yes?"

And then there was his smile, an impossibly bright grin that slowly spread across his face and lit up the world. A smile I felt in my *thighs* (months later, velcroed to each other in the dark, he said that when he started receiving my packages before my first day, my name randomly called to mind a "lumpy judge-y church girl," so he was delighted I was me). I couldn't help but smile back, and then we were just grinning at each other for a second for no good reason.

"So," he said, "is that shirt like a fashion thing, or are you a real Prince fan?"

"Ha! Little boy, you have no idea."

"Prove it."

Prove it? We launched into a Prince-off, and I realized that his obsession *almost* eclipsed mine (i.e., Halloween costumes, wearing "slave" on his cheek to elementary school, a totally decorative Purple Rain-esque white guitar). And that was that. I had someone to talk about obscure shit no one else cared about!

I started emailing him Prince bootlegs, and then the conversation broadened and we realized we had a scary number of other things in common. We *thought* the same. We loved and hated the same things. (Who was it who said, "It's not what you're like, it's what you like?") And I could be weird around him! Men usually don't want weird from pretty girls; that's not part of the package. But he expected it, 'cause he was weird, too. This is a person who imagines that a voiceover's narrating his life, like in *The Wonder Years*. He had a cat named Adam—in honor of the Counting Crows' Adam Duritz, who he inexplicably loved as a kid. The cat is female, by the way.

And yet for all we had in common, we were totally exotic to each other. He was from a tough section of Brooklyn, and I grew up in an upper-middle-class DC suburb. It was constantly story time—we were ravenous for vignettes from each other's lives. He couldn't believe my life, that I'd lived all over the world and written books, hosted a radio show, and been on TV.

"Admit it," he would later murmur into my hair one night, half asleep, "you're secretly the Princess of Zamunda."

He couldn't believe my life—and I didn't know how he made it out of his alive. I also found it hard to think about his story without feeling a tremendous amount of anger and sadness. He was always the smartest kid in his class—a writer, too—the one who was supposed to make it, the one who stayed focused and got into college.

But after a string of financial mishaps, he had to drop out. He got into a new university the following year, and the same thing happened. And now he was working in the mailroom.

We could not stop talking to each other over email, on the phone, in clandestine corners—all day, all night, like teenagers. I'd known him a month and we were suddenly best friends. Friends who shamelessly and indulgently flirted in my office (thank God I had a door).

My heels got higher and my skirts got shorter. My sister met me at the office one day for lunch and met him, and later accused me of "wagging my hips" at him. Wagging my hips? I suddenly felt like this voluptuous, totally sensual creature. I felt my heretofore totally flat ass get plumper as a symptom of the weight of my obsession. I never would've believed that I could behave this way at work. I also never thought it would go any further than our crazy-chatty obsession and dangerously delicious crushing—because, well, this is where my bougie snobbery comes in. The "upstairs, downstairs" of it all. As much as I adored him, this kid couldn't possibly have the balls to ask *me* out. I mean, come on.

But he did. And I said yes. And I'd like to formally apologize to a certain dimly lit Soho restaurant for behaving in a manner unbecoming a Southern belle. After that night, we were inseparable. We wanted nothing more than to get advanced degrees in each other. No agenda but *l'amour*. Anaïs Nin said some men filled all her gaps, while others only emphasized her loneliness. He was a gap-filler (ahem). It's like I'd misplaced my "oomph" somewhere in '07, and he'd found it in the back of a cab, dusted it off, and dragged it to my doorstep wrapped in a crimson bow.

———

At first, the work thing made it even sexier. No one could know about the two of us, because it was way too scandalous. So all day long, we pretended not to be crazy about each other, which heightened the whole thing. For two highly dramatic people who lived in a world of movies and music, this was so rich.

Until it wasn't anymore. Until it all settled down and he was just my boyfriend. And I wanted to talk about what you did over the weekend with your coworkers, but I couldn't. And I had to run out of a movie theater because the fashion editor from my website just walked in. But none of that mattered, because we felt so dazed and lucky that we had found these unlikely soul mates in each other. We went *all out!* We loved each other in an idealized, unconditionally worshipful kind of way. We wanted to save each other, always. When I was laid off on December 15 with two weeks' severance, he showed up at my house with a Christmas tree, groceries, and a budget. He wasn't sure how to start writing professionally, so I introduced him to a *Huffington Post* editor, and he landed a weekly blog. He was my angel, and I wanted to be his. The odds were already so stacked against us that we never wanted to argue, never wanted to bring any-thing unsavory into the relationship.

Tough to sustain in the real world, I know. You kinda need to wake up on a Tuesday in bad pajamas, fight about who's supposed to change the kitty litter, and then delete his DVR queue just to be shitty.

Only eighth-graders and J. Lo believe you can live on love. We talked about everything except for the obvious, which was that it was never going to work. We were in such vastly different places that it could never be a practical, marriage-and-babies thing. We had no idea what to do with each other, outside of each other. We barely even went anywhere. We'd just hang out at my apartment in our own little bubble. Our worlds were drastically different... and outside of my apartment, we felt it. There was no getting around it. We were safe on my couch, so that's where we stayed.

In the end, it had to end. Breaking up was unbearable—why were we given this great love if we couldn't be together?—but stay-ing together was holding us back from the rest of our lives, in a way. One day I'll look back on it through sepia-tinted lenses, all wistful eyes and faraway smile, fondly remembering my transformative love affair. He reminded me who I was, nudged me into loving myself again—maybe for the first time, if I'm all-the-way honest. But today? It just hurts. It's an ocean of ache.

I feel hopeful about the future. I've been on a few dates with age-appropriate men, and they've been dashing and interesting, but they're not him (and I'm suddenly affronted by middle-aged midsections). I know I'll never be loved like that again, with that openness and willingness. He'd never loved before, and no one had ever hurt him. I hope no one ever does.

—**Tia Williams**

Tia Williams is a former beauty editor for Elle, Glamour, Lucky, *and* Essence.com. *Williams is also the author of* The Accidental Diva, It Chicks, Sixteen Candles, *and Iman's* The Beauty of Color. *She recently relaunched her award-winning blog,* Shake Your Beauty.

CHAPTER 3

And Still There Is Hope

I GREW UP THE ELDEST OF FIVE IN A TWO-PARENT FAMILY IN Milwaukee, Wisconsin. My father was a Baptist minister and my mother was a teacher. I actually believed that everyone grew up the way that I did, in an "intact" home. My parents were close and very loving toward one another. I thought for the longest time that my mother's first name was Dear, because that's what my father called her.

I grew up with the expectation that I would marry someday and have a family. The values instilled in me made me understand that sex outside of marriage or becoming a teen mom were absolutely not an option! It was also a given that I would go to college and meet my future husband. I dated a guy in high school but was saving myself sexually for marriage.

I attended Northwestern University in Evanston, Illinois, where there were a plethora of men whom I deemed "husband material." My freshman year, I dated several guys, but all of the relationships were nonsexual. The summer after my freshman year, I had my first sexual experience. The guy was a blue-collar worker and a coworker of a friend of mine. He dared me to have sex with him and said he'd had a vasectomy so there was no concern about pregnancy. I was 19, naïve, and I believed him! When I returned to school in the fall, I discovered that I had become pregnant from my first sexual encounter.

I was shocked. I called the guy. He admitted that he lied to me about the vasectomy because he wanted me to get pregnant so we would have to get married! I faced a serious conflict with my values: having premarital sex *and* getting pregnant! What would my parents think? What would the people from church think? How could I disappoint my parents, my family, my church? What kind of example was I setting for my younger siblings? I was filled with shame!

I proceeded with an abortion. Abortions were illegal then, so I had to go to a "back-alley" place. I ended up lying on the dining room table of someone's home in the Chicago neighborhood of Hyde Park. I was blindfolded. I never saw who performed the procedure and knew nothing of their qualifications. It was a really terrible experience. I know that God really had to be looking out for me to see me through it.

I was so fed up with men that I didn't date anyone for almost a year after that experience. There was a guy who was persistent and wanted to date me, but because he didn't meet my superficial standard of being at least six feet tall I didn't give him the time of day (he later became a VP of a major corporation). Then I met a Nigerian guy who was studying engineering, and we dated my last two years of college. One Christmas break, he came home with me, and as soon as we sat down to dinner my mother asked how many wives he planned to have (she knew his father had two). She wanted to make it clear that if I married him, I would be the *only* wife. Imagine my surprise when a wife materialized at graduation! He had been dating me and had a wife back home in Nigeria the whole time!

After graduation, I went to medical school in Madison, Wisconsin. What better place than medical school for me to meet my future husband? There was a cadre of about 16 African-American students, and one man in particular caught my eye. He had been a 4.0 student prior to attending Madison. He was highly sought after and had been accepted at Harvard Medical School. Not only was he very intelligent, but he was handsome as well: six-foot-two with amazing dimples! I thought he had perfect husband potential, so I tirelessly pursued him. Since he was in the class behind me, I made myself available to orient him to the school and campus. I was very friendly and always around when he was studying in the library. We became friends and started going on study dates. Most of our "dates" were actually study dates. We transitioned into a couple and were married a year later.

I had the responsibility of doing *all* of the housework in our marriage (even though I was in medical school too). He had the luxury of spending all of his time studying. I had grown up with old-school traditional values, where wives obeyed their husbands. Whatever he requested, I complied with, down to how I dressed. He felt that women shouldn't wear pants, so there I was in Madison, Wisconsin, walking around in subzero temperatures wearing dresses and skirts because that was what he wanted. When it came time to choose where we did our residencies, he wanted to go to New York, but I wanted to go to California. He said to me, "If you want to be married to me, you have to go to New York." Being the obedient wife I was, we went to New York.

Our son was born during the first year of my psychiatry residency, which is when things really started to fall apart. There was infidelity and physical abuse, so I filed for divorce. I spent the next three years of my residency going through a divorce and a child custody battle. He didn't offer any financial support. New York was expensive on top of the legal fees, so in addition to spending between 60 and 80 hours doing my residency, I moonlighted at hospitals in Brooklyn and Staten Island so I could pay the bills and babysitters. I became stressed and depressed. I started going to psychotherapy three times a week, both so I could be whole and so I could properly help my patients. I did this throughout my entire residency.

The finalization of the divorce coincided with the end of my residency. I decided to return home to Milwaukee because my family was there and could provide moral support and help me raise my child. The night before I left New York for Madison, I talked to my ex. He took responsibility for the dissolution of our marriage. He admitted that he had a problem with us both pursuing medicine. He said he felt that he had to compete with me. I didn't feel a sense of competition, but he did. He admitted that the reason he'd insisted I do all of the housework in medical school was to take away from my study time so that I wouldn't be able to perform as well as him. He said that he felt that if we were both doctors, I wouldn't put him on a pedestal and idolize him. He wanted a woman who would worship him because he was an MD. He admitted to all of this *after* the dissolution of the marriage. A few months after I returned to Milwaukee, my ex-husband was found dead from a heroin and cocaine overdose. I had no idea he was using during our marriage.

I spent a few years in Milwaukee and eventually moved to Atlanta. I had several relationships. I found myself gravitating to African men, because I felt that there wasn't a sufficient pool of African-American men who met my standards of education and world travel. I even dated a man 20 years my junior. He was working on his PhD in math at Georgia Tech and was very serious about our relationship. He wanted to marry. I felt comfortable in the relationship until my teenage son asked, "How old is he? He's closer to my age than yours."

After that, I told my friend that he should find someone younger so he could have children. (I was in my forties at the time.) He was devastated. A few years ago, I wondered what happened to him and found out that he was teaching at a university in Canada, married with a daughter.

I tried to be less restrictive about my educational standards for dating. One day, I was in Home Depot buying flowers and I met a handsome, tall, and dark-skinned contractor buying supplies. We flirted; he asked if he could take me to dinner and a movie. I never told him what my occupation was. When it was time for the date, he came to my house to pick me up. He walked through the front door of my Buckhead home, his eyes surveying the room. He remarked, "I can't date you! You are way out of my league." Then he turned and walked out the front door!

My dating experience has ranged from men wanting me to be a Sugar Mama to guys who felt like they were not up to par because of our differences in education or income. Although I have always told my patients with similar challenges to expand their options by dating outside their race, I have never done so myself. I don't know what it is, but I have some type of inner taboo that prevents me from doing it. Caucasian men have approached me on several occasions. I remember in medical school, my anatomy partner, a former football player, kept asking me out. I couldn't go there! When I was doing my residency in New York, one of my fellow residents kept asking me out. I declined. Later I learned that he married an African-American woman.

I have also encouraged my patients to try online dating. I wouldn't recommend it if I hadn't tried it myself. There are caveats to online dating. People can be dishonest. I advise my patients do to a background check. I had an experience with a man who presented himself in one manner, but a background check revealed a 20-page dossier that included incarcerations and felonies. I forwarded this information to the dating site and they removed him from the database.

I'm currently involved in an eight-month relationship with a man eight years my junior. We met online and he pursued me. His background is in social services and education. I didn't list my profession, and he didn't have a photo. Honestly, if he had posted his photo I would *not* have responded since he has cornrows and diamond earrings! That is definitely *not* the look I have gone for in the past. He really is a nice guy, and we have great compatibility and role flexibility. Cooking is not my forte, but he is excellent at it and takes pride in preparing meals. He would clean my house and do my laundry if I allowed him to! (I pay someone to do those things.) He says it is "what real men do."

Initially, he worried that I would leave him for another doctor. His family reinforced this insecurity. What makes our relationship work is that we are best friends and one another's biggest fan. I have an optimistic view of relationships and marriage in the African American community. I believe in the metaphysical laws of attraction: If you are being positive and putting out positive energy, you will attract a person with a positive attitude. I feel very hopeful.

Even though I am a psychiatrist, I have still experienced the same challenges as most African-American women. What I've learned in exclusively dating black men is that you have to exercise flexibility. You can't just look at what they do or how much they make; you have to look at the person. When I was younger, I put a lot of emphasis on their academic and material status; now I look at the person, his individual traits, and his character. Whenever I meet a new man, I always ask myself if he is nurturing and if we are compatible, rather than focusing on the superficial.

I think relationships in the African-American community are challenging because we still have a lot of residual effects of slavery. This has fostered a lot of distrust between men and women, and it contributes to the lack of respect we show each other. In popular black culture, women call men "dogs" and men call women "hoes"— you get my point. What I now know is: In order to get respect from others, you must respect yourself. A lot of black women and men suffer from low self-esteem. It should come as no surprise that if we don't respect ourselves, we can't expect to anyone else to respect us.

We need to learn the skills to deal with personal growth, relationships, and marriage, because most of us are out here winging it. We need to change the images being presented about marriage and relationships in the African American community and focus on the positive attributes. We need to better understand our expectations of marriage so that we can strengthen our community.

—**Cassandra Wanzo, MD**

Cassandra Wanzo, MD, received her undergraduate degree from Northwestern University. She attended medical school at the University of Wisconsin and completed her psychiatric residency at Saint Vincent's Medical Center in New York City. Wanzo is a diplomate of the American Board of Psychiatry and Neurology. She is in private practice in Atlanta and believes in treating the whole person with dignity and respect.

CHAPTER 4

Back to (Single) Life

O N THE MORNING OF AUGUST 10, 2010, I STOOD IN FRONT OF a judge with my lawyer by my side. I was getting divorced. When I'd gotten married seven years earlier—ironically, on the same date—I never imagined that I'd find myself in that position. But there I was, in a courtroom, divvying up assets and putting an end to my marriage.

August 10, 2003 was a Sunday. I was 54 years old, and as I walked down the aisle for the first time, I knew that it was a moment my family and friends probably never thought they'd see. Because I'd lived all of my life as a single man, nobody could believe that I was getting married. They didn't believe that I wasn't nervous either, but I wasn't—at all. I was cool, actually. I was happy and felt that I was making the right decision. I was also looking forward to sharing my life with my soon-to-be wife. My retirement plans were set for the following summer, and she was on schedule to retire shortly after, so we were excited about the prospect of traveling and creating new experiences together. We wanted to enjoy each other's company and just *be,* just flow. The timing felt right. Timing is key.

Although I got married later in life, I wasn't necessarily opposed to marriage. I didn't have any fantasies about what I thought the institution represented either. Based on my upbringing and the relationships I'd had and witnessed over the years, I think I had a pretty straightforward outlook going in. To me, marriage is about partnership. It means having someone to hold your hand, watch your back, and assist you through the maze of life. It's an exercise in give-and-take that requires balance from both ends. That being said, I was also aware that marriage means different things for different people at different times in their lives.

When people get married young, they're still trying to figure out who they are as individuals. The hope is that there will be room for each person to grow along the way. There are also marriages based on financial gain, and some that involve people looking outside of themselves to fill emotional and spiritual voids. I understand and respect those scenarios, but as you get older and develop a better sense of who you are, there is a level of acceptance that comes into play when you're seeking a partner. That's the space I was in when I met my now ex-wife eleven years ago. But I'm getting ahead of myself.

I grew up with my mother and older sister. Though my parents were married, I don't really remember much of their time together because my father left the family early. When I was five years old and my sister was seven, my mother moved us from an apartment in Brooklyn to a two-family house in Queens and raised us on her own. She was the only single mother on our block, but I didn't think anything of it at the time. I never felt that I was lacking anything.

Aside from my aunts and uncles and some of my friends' parents, I don't remember being exposed to many examples of marriage during my childhood. Perhaps the major difference between my family and two-parent families was money. In hindsight, I'm sure having two incomes would have made things easier for us, but as a kid, none of that really mattered. I had my mother, my sister, and our dog, so I was good. Life was good.

Many people believe that mothers raise their daughters and coddle their sons. That wasn't the case in our house. My mother led by example and instilled in us the value of being independent. We took care of the dog and did our share of household chores, although my sister would do almost anything to get out of washing the dishes. My mother insisted that we practice our penmanship and I remember a game she played with us when we were really young where we'd recite the alphabet as she typed each letter on the typewriter. Let's just say that she was quick on the keyboard. She taught us to be responsible and made sure that we knew how to take care of ourselves. I left her house knowing how to cook, clean, iron, and sew.

By the time I was in my early 20s, I was done with school and had served my time in the Army after the draft. While I was trying to find my way as a young man, some of my friends started pairing off and getting married. I remember thinking, *Good for them.* I wasn't on that page. Nowhere near it. Thinking back, I'm sure I thought that marriage was a possibility for me, but it was something that was far off in the very distant future. I was too busy ripping and running the streets and having a good time. There was a lot of dating and partying going on then. I was just doing my thing.

I've often been described as a serial monogamist, but I didn't really think of myself that way. I've never been the type of person who believed that the end of a relationship meant the end of my life, even after a painful breakup. There were a couple of times when I thought I'd found The One, but for whatever reason, things didn't work out. When it came down to what I was looking for in a woman, I really wanted to be with someone who could accept me as I was and allow me to be me. I'd like to think that I was a good partner. I wasn't one to try to take anything from anybody or be slick. I've always been a laid-back kind of guy, but back then I wasn't as stable and committed as my girlfriends wanted me to be. For that, I blame youth.

As I got older and more of my friends got married, I noticed a shift. I didn't feel a need to be a part of "the club," but I think my single-guy status became a problem, especially for some of the wives. Whether they were trying to set me up with their single girlfriends or, in a few instances, making subtle passes at me themselves, I often felt too eligible. I also felt as though they looked at me with distrustful eyes because they feared that I'd be a bad influence on their husbands. Many times, it was uncomfortable for me to spend time with my married friends because my bachelorhood was such an issue.

From the outside looking in, I can imagine that my life seemed like a dream come true to some people. Because I wasn't married and didn't have children, my time was my own. While I certainly enjoyed the benefits of single life, it wasn't always as easy as it looked. Nobody really understood that part of the equation, though. For starters, when you're single, everything depends on you. There's that old saying, "If you want to dance to the music, you have to pay the band," and to that I've always countered, "Yeah, I'm going to pay the band *and* write the lyrics, sing the song, and play the instruments, too. I *am* the show."

Life is about tradeoffs. Yes, I had my freedom, but when it came to finding the focus and energy to progress or having the strength to endure hardships, I was on my own, too. Moving forward professionally, spiritually, and financially required my full attention. If I wanted something—whether it was a promotion, a new car, or even a piece of property—I had to think it over, nurture the idea, plot it out, and then massage it again. I did all of that by myself, for years, and although it was stressful at times, I'd like to think that it made me stronger. I didn't feel incomplete because I wasn't married. I was a whole person, someone who had a lot of love and experience to share with the right person.

My ex-wife and I met in the fall of 2001 in a tax preparation class. I can't remember who spoke to whom first, but once we started talking, the conversation was easy. Our initial conversations were related to the class and soon after, we started talking to each other about ourselves. Two weeks after we met, we went on our first date.

It was nice to learn that we had some things in common. We were close in age (I was six months older), and like me, she was nearing the end of her working days. On the flip side, she had been married before. Twice. She was also the mother of a grown son and daughter and had a young grandson, too. I could hear from her stories that her journey had not always been easy, and what I came to appreciate about her in those early days was that she had lived a full life. She'd overcome difficult times, too, which showed me that she had a certain level of strength and perseverance. That, I could appreciate. Aside from what I liked about her, it felt good to know that she genuinely liked me.

We dated for two years and lived separately until we got married. During that time, we began to learn about our differences, too. For example, the branches on my family tree weren't as extensive as her branches, which included siblings and children and aunts and uncles and cousins and nieces and nephews and a grandchild. Coming from a small family and having a tight-knit circle of longtime friends, I wasn't used to having so much activity buzzing around me all of the time. Whether her phone was ringing off the hook or we were socializing amongst a house full of folks at weekly get-togethers, there was always something going on. That took some getting used to, but I enjoyed going along for the ride. Her people were easygoing and always seemed to have a good time together. They welcomed me with open arms and my friends and family did the same for her.

Speaking of family, I'll never forget something that her aunt told us after we announced our engagement. It was such a simple statement and these many years later, I still remember the very moment she said, "Now, don't go trying to change each other." No truer words have ever been spoken.

The first sign of trouble was when she started keeping tabs. We'd been married for a few months when I got the feeling that she was tracking me. It seemed harmless at first, but as we settled into our first year of marriage, she was clocking my every move. If I wasn't home when she walked through the door, she'd call my cell phone immediately. Rather than saying, "Hello," or asking about my day, her first question was always, "Where are you?" It didn't matter if I was at the barbershop or riding my bike in the park. She was rarely satisfied with my answer. That wasn't anything I'd experienced when we were dating, so her behavior seemed odd. When we first started seeing each other, I'd call to tell her that I was hanging out and she had no problem. The running joke was, "I'm driving to Vegas and I'll be back in the morning." I know it sounds like a cliché, but once we got married, that all changed. Everything changed.

From my standpoint, there was no reason for her to be suspicious. I didn't understand her motives, mainly because her sudden distrust of me was so unwarranted. She had activities that she enjoyed doing alone, or with friends, and I thought it was great that she had her own thing going on. I never thought to make her accountable for each moment that we were apart, but she didn't give me that consideration. Over time, I was annoyed by her constant inquisitions and accusations, which, of course, caused dissent at home. Her attempts to monitor my movements were just the tip of the iceberg, yet part of me just couldn't believe what was happening.

She often referred to herself as the "Lady of the House," which I found interesting because she didn't do much around the house. Since I was accustomed to living alone, I'd always kept a neat house, yet she rarely lifted a finger. I'm not suggesting that either of us were tied to specific duties based on gender, nor was I keeping a checklist of who did what, but I soon realized that aside from grocery shopping, which we did together, I was doing everything from watering the flowers and cutting the grass to scrubbing the bathroom tiles, and anything in between. I'd been used to doing all of those things as a single man, but as a married man, I asked myself, "Wait, I thought we were in this together? What happened to our partnership?"

I didn't have inflated expectations when we got married, so I figured that we were just having some growing pains. That's to be expected, right? So, instead of allowing the tension to escalate, I made a conscious decision to stay calm and take things in stride. Whenever we were out with other couples and someone asked how things were going, I'd say, "Oh, this is all new for me, so I'm still reading the manual. Right now, I'm on chapter 'Let it Go.'" That answer always kept the mood light and got people laughing and honestly, that's exactly what I was trying to do—just let it go, let it roll off.

As time progressed, it became obvious that she was not only trying to change me, but control and diminish me as well. When we made joint purchases for the house, she'd ask for my input, which, in the end, didn't hold much weight. In reality, she was more concerned about keeping up with the Joneses and comparing notes with her girlfriends. Again, I tried to stay calm, but things took a turn for the worse when we decided to do some remodeling. To make a long story short, after the basement was finished, she started chastising me for spending too much time downstairs. I could not wrap my head around the fact that the same person who was constantly questioning my whereabouts when I left the house was now telling me which rooms I could occupy—or not—when I was *in* the house. It was at that point that my patience really started wearing thin.

By the time we reached our fourth anniversary, we were in bad shape. The resentment in the air was thick, but whenever I tried to sit down to talk things over, I was faced with instant hostility. I'm not much of an arguer, but she would rant and rave for hours and make idle threats, which caused me to shut down. I'll never know how we got to that point so quickly and although I really loved and cared for her, I didn't know how to fix things. It seemed that her actions were based in insecurity, which was another thing that I hadn't picked up on when we were dating. When I finally reached out to some friends for advice, they asked if I'd noticed any signs before we got married. Not only had I not noticed any of this before, I didn't know where it was coming from now.

As much as I didn't want our marriage to end, I really couldn't see how things could improve. I tried to hold on to the hope that, if we could at least keep talking, maybe we might reach a point of understanding. My efforts fell short because each time I tried to talk to her, the conversation started and ended with an argument. Then one night, she screamed, "Call my lawyer!" That's when I knew we'd reached the end of the road.

When the lawyers got involved, I realized that she intended to fight dirty until the bitter end. Though I was willing to be fair, she wanted *everything*—including the house, which I'd purchased on my own back in 1998. I'd added her name to the deed in 2004. She'd told me stories about not having that kind of security in her previous marriages, so I wanted her to feel at ease. I was more than happy to do it, but I came to regret that decision. She also wanted all of the furniture that we'd purchased together, as well as the dishes and silverware. If battling for two years wasn't exhausting enough, we also lived in the house together until the details were settled. In the end, I managed to keep the house, but it cost me.

I was at a point in my life where I could overcome a breakup a lot faster than when I was in my twenties, thirties, and forties. Once I accepted that the marriage was beyond repair, I really had no problem with the idea of returning to single life. I knew that I'd be okay, because what meant the most to me was having peace. No matter what I'd ever had to deal with out in the world, I was always able to find solace when I arrived home and locked the door behind me. It wasn't until I got married that I felt so much stress and angst at home. In retrospect, I can honestly say that I was just as content on the day that we got married as I was on the day our divorce was finalized. The only thing I wish I'd done differently would be to start the divorce proceedings sooner, before things got so ugly.

Since officially parting ways with my ex-wife in July 2011, many people have asked if I'd ever remarry. The answer is yes. But just like when I announced that I was getting married the first time, nobody can believe that I would try it again. Rather than be bitter, I take the experience for what it was. I also accept half of the blame, because I know that it takes two to tango. I'm sorry that things didn't work out, yet I've chosen to accept the lessons and keep living.

Today, at 63, I'm enjoying my life again, as a single man. I'm in a new relationship and we're taking it slow. She has her own place and I have mine, and there's no pressure, no rush, from either side. The two of us travel as often as we can, and I must say that retirement is treating me quite well. I'm in a good place.

I don't have regrets about my first marriage, nor do I feel any shame about being divorced. Instead, I'm glad that I was able to find my way back to myself. I firmly believe that there's always more on the other side. Life goes on, *I've* moved on… and I'm happy.

—Al Farnell

Al Farnell served as manager of safety and health at the United States Postal Service until his retirement in 2004. A native New Yorker and lifelong sports enthusiast, Farnell now fills his free time with long-distance cycling and paddleball. "Back to (Single) Life" is his first published essay.

CHAPTER 5

Love Is Not the Enemy

"IT'S OKAY NOT TO LOVE THEIR CHILDREN." I'LL NEVER FORGET that line out of a random book I found on the bottom shelf of the Child and Family Psychology section of a mainstream bookstore, over a decade ago. I sat down and cried in the aisle.

I was living in Atlanta, Georgia. I'd moved there in 2000 after a large outdoor wedding at the Cloisters in upper Manhattan. Don Babatunde from the Last Poets summoned the ancestors with drums. Imani Uzuri sang. There were dancers. The flower children were dream hampton's and pianist Marc Carey's daughters. I had my best man in town to stand beside my first husband and close friend, Sharrif Simmons, his brothers, his friends, and two of my five biological brothers. My bridesmaids wore orange sari fabric from India. I rocked a matching veil adorned with cowrie shells. Our Memorial Day wedding was Poetic African/Eastern Chic. We were quite inspired by the Earth, Wind, & Fire box set. I found my cream-colored, fitted, lace-trimmed dress with a train in a magazine and bought it on Fifth Avenue. We had a jam session after the wedding, we rode a limo up St. Nicholas Avenue, and Saul Williams did the robot down the aisle. I think we danced to Michael Jackson for our first dance. "Billie Jean."

"Mommy and Daddy are getting married!"

We had been famous poets in love, with a toddler son in tow, in New York City just a few years before I found myself broken on the floor of that bookstore, searching for support for a loss that apparently did not exist. The lack of resources for women who love and date men with children from prior relationships was a deep revelation for me, considering how many women of color I know who date men with children.

When I met Sharrif, he was tall and handsome, with long locks and a beautiful smile. A new arrival from Detroit, I was getting to know some of the future infamous writers and poets in the '90s New York City art scene. I was still on the open mic list at Brooklyn Moon Café, and a mutual artist friend insisted that we meet. We became fast friends and shared an admiration of each other's work. We both loved to dance, laughed often, and loved reading and talking about revolutionary writers who had shaped us. The first night we met, he had to leave early to begin the short walk to his Fort Greene apartment. He had a brand new baby boy at home named Omari.

When I met him, my future sun, my life was so full of light. I'm convinced my name lies in some ancient text somewhere. Jessica is Hebrew for "rich," and I would update the definition further with "Somebody's mommy, for God's sake!" When I became a mother for the first time, a secret joy would fill up my days.

In the beginning, being a mommy was something I would only share with my three-year-old son, Omari. Our relationship was fun, an innocent love that happened organically, without judgment or baby shower gifts, no "welcome to the family" announcements, no paperwork. Omari Jazz. He was so beautiful, with a sweet, wet smile and personality beyond his years. Blood had nothing to do with this adorable yellow-brown boy quickly becoming my family. His eyes were deep and brown, and he trusted me.

Sharrif took him literally everywhere. I loved that family energy of the New York City art scene. Having children was an extension of our lives. We could be out-loud parents, and we'd just pass the babies around or wrap them around our bodies and keep performing. He was being raised around a young, hip artist community, but I became more mommy-protective of Omari the closer we got.

I was still driving my very Detroit purple Ford pick-up truck and learning the subway system when my life changed in 1995, when I appeared on *Showtime at the Apollo*. I remember Sharrif telling me he'd taped the performances on his VHS recorder. We had become comrades, dance partners, and confidantes during my first six months in Brooklyn. I was close enough to Sharrif to be one of

Omari's regular babysitters when he had shows. My boyfriend at the time and I would hang with Omari so Sharrif could have a break. Sharrif and I were kindred spirits, but it was truly a friendship. My intentions with Omari were organic and loving.

I remember when things began falling apart for Sharrif and his family. Omari's biological mom had been diagnosed with acute paranoid schizophrenia, and her ability to care for Omari was slipping away. I was supportive of Sharrif through this very difficult time in his life. No dad expects to have to step in and care for a new baby the way a mother is expected to with ease. I didn't realize I was nurturing a future bond with Omari, but I did love Sharrif dearly as a friend. Ultimately, that meant loving his son just as much, if not more.

And I did.

I was 23, single, and a full-time poet in New York City. I was dating and flirting with a few different artists, including Dante Smith, the young man who would become the very famous Mos Def. I got serious with a filmmaker and poet named Pierre Bonnett, and he moved into my Brooklyn brownstone with me for a while until we decided to move to Harlem together. I needed a break from Brooklyn. I was quickly becoming a well-known artist, and the lack of privacy was overwhelming as my Fort Greene neighborhood became increasingly popular.

Harlem reminded me more of my upbringing and the Motown-Dobbs-hat-daddy-cool energy of Detroit. I've learned that every decision in life (conscious and unconscious) is connected to the next move your life makes. I thought I was moving to New York to find my voice as a poet, when I was really going to meet my earth son and become a full-time mommy.

I moved to Sugar Hill, around the corner from cool artists like Cassandra Wilson and writer/musician Greg Tate. Tate was serendipitously playing host to Sharrif and baby Omari while Sharrif was getting his footing and still fighting for full legal custody of his two-year-old son.

I thought I was moving to Harlem to start my life with my boyfriend. That relationship ended soon after the move, and I invited my single-father friend to move into my three-bedroom apartment. I wanted to give Omari his own room. I went to IKEA and bought him a bed and a table and dressers. I wanted to give him the world and nothing less, like any other mom.

There was never a separation from Sharrif and his precocious, beautiful son. Motherhood was a matter of responsibility. I was raised in a typical Western-thinking household, but my approach to life and loving the men in my life was more communal, less Brady Bunch, more Chinua Achebe village. I needed broader definitions of love for the capacity of my heart. I never wanted a special award or recognition for loving my son. I simply loved a man who had a child who needed a mom, and I thought that was enough.

It wasn't.

Becoming a mother when you are not a birth mom does not include baby showers or well wishers. You are sometimes looked upon as a thief, and you have to be strong enough to fight off your own second guesses about simply loving your family.

Omari was the glue that held us together. We had to fight to be together. I remember when Omari began calling me Mommy for the first time. He was so intuitive about other people that he would only do it in private, or when he felt safe. "Mommy?!" he would call and ask me at the same time. And I always answered without hesitation.

Sharrif was a longtime New Yorker, and I was performing on stages I'd only dreamt about—the Schomburg Center for Research in Black Culture, Central Park Summerstage, the Theater at Madison Square Garden, and the Apollo Theater. And then we decided to move to Atlanta after we were married. There was no artistic reason for me to move. I left New York City for my Omari. For my son. For peace of mind for my family. The move would eventually lead to the end of our marriage, which needed the nurturing of art and community more than we realized.

I wanted Omari to have a "normal" life. I wanted to be his mommy freely, without discerning, jealous glances from outsiders. Without worrying about being verbally attacked by his biological mother after one of my appearances. It was a struggle to simply openly love my earth son, who loved me and more importantly, needed me.

Moving is an important part of my makeup. I am a gypsy woman, and all health-related illnesses associated with the stress of moving are definitely embedded beneath my skin. When you are a woman, sometimes you have to move. When you are an artist, it's necessary. When you are a mom, it's not so easy.

Especially when your baby isn't coming with you.

I wrote poems to help me find comfort, since there were no books, no support groups, no real friends or family who truly understood how I felt.

Biology Lesson: Poem for Omari

I sit inside my life as an observer
I boil tea and count the steps
I never noticed them before now.
Next week they will be red and royal.
Fat-lipped for someone's feet to step on.

The wonder of poetry and explanation
Politics and love seem so contrary
I rehearse a smile and leave for the panel
I entertain guests. I watch them watch me.
I listen to phone calls from friends who
Never call to check for my heart.
Everything is a lie. Everything is the truth.

I bake his favorite macaroni and cheese.
I make his bed, purchase a twin
Spiderman comforter with sheets and pillowcases.
They still smell new.

You loved them and flopped down and smiled
When you came to visit.
No math, no parenting, just visit.
I'm unfamiliar with this song.
Strange fruit. A mango in winter.
This was your house. Our house.

Some say I should make it my
workout center
meditation room
second office.

You want bunk beds for your 8th birthday.

I think about the Bible story
I'm actually referring to the Bible here.
The one about the two mothers
Fighting over a child. A boy.
One mother who agrees to allow the boy
To be cut in two to please both sides.
The real mother walks away and decides
To allow the child his life
Even if it is without her.
Today I tried to do that with you
And I think you knew it.
On the Upper West Side
I actually tried to not call for the
Third day in a row.
I was giving up. I was giving into a selfish world
Doing what others told me to do

Just let go.
Just have your "own" children.
Just stop loving your son.

You told me you loved me and missed me
Over and over that day.
Promised to come see me next month.
You wanted to know where I was

Exactly!

I'm crying in Starbucks on the Upper West Side
The His/Herstory film crew just called.
I'm at the wrong one.
How can there be so many coffee shops
On one block.
This entire city is sedated.

This is my life.

I think of us slow dancing in the kitchen
You falling asleep on my stomach.
Your magnet science experiment winning first place.
You are all glitter and gold and

"I'm fine, mommy"

And missing.
You have been my reason for wanting to be
A better person, a responsible mother
A good parent, a wife, a teacher.
You helped me fall in love.
I never needed the courts or legal documents
To love you.
I can't explain to you the madness of grownups
Why I wasn't invited for the holidays.
Why we can't spend certain days together anymore.
Why Mommy can't do your homework with you
When she helped you learn to read and write and spell.
You have political artistic parents who talk about
The war, the government and all kinds of deep things.
But can't revolutionize loving you apart.
How will we divide the days?
The equation is complicated.
I hate math. I always will.
You remind me of all the times you would chase me
Around the house with open jars of pickled herring

I am not a fish
You are my love child
You make me laugh in places
I've never smiled.

No one understood why I fell into a depression; why I felt abandoned, even betrayed; or why I went into a mourning from which
I am still recovering, all over the loss of a child I did not make and
who wasn't dead.

To this day, my raising Omari is referred to by others as "practice." Something I should put behind me and move on. I kept being
told I'd have more kids that would replace him eventually. When I
was fighting for visitation rights, I was asked, "Is Omari really with
all the trouble? Is he worth the energy of the fight?"

The answer was absolutely, yes.

When I committed myself to Sharrif as his wife, I also committed to being his son's mom. I never looked at that as temporary,
and I was too naïve and dreamy to follow our lawyer's advice and
get full parental rights by adopting Omari. I didn't think it would
be necessary. It's one of my biggest regrets and personal failures as a
parent. I've written my son apology letters he's never read. I didn't
know it was necessary to empower myself in the event of a divorce
from Omari's dad. I thought love was enough, and it would never be
a matter of courts or intangible laws. I never needed a court to love
my son and never wanted to have to prove my rights as a mother
this way.

Stepmoms/earth moms often go beyond what's normal to prove
themselves as good parents, as worthy of respect as a parent.

This was a time where I often wondered, "where did the love
go?"

When Omari was 11, I was pregnant with my first biological
son, King. I cried my entire first trimester, longing to see my older
son, who wasn't allowed to see me for my entire pregnancy. I lost
Omari in ways that made me regret walking away from my failing
marriage. I never imagined not having him for visits or not being
his mom. I kept his room intact for years until I moved into a new

home and married my second husband, who came with two sons and a daughter.

"Love is not the enemy" became my mantra.

I don't know why I didn't run in the other direction of any man with kids, after being so devastated by the loss of Omari. I loved children and never looked down on men or women for giving birth, as long as they were taking care of their responsibilities. I loved my stepchildren and we spent weekends and vacations together, and I became close to them. They knew Omari as my son, and eventually Omari was around less frequently.

After a devastating affair, I left my second husband at the end of 2007 and returned home to Detroit to rebuild my life with King.

I don't regret the men I've loved or the children I've loved through them. I do believe there should be more support for women who marry men who already have children. It takes a lot to get past the drama, to be mature enough to take your personal emotions or jealousies out of the equation, and to be able to create a loving environment for the children in your lives.

How many men over thirty do you know without any children?

In 2012, my handsome 17-year-old son Omari Jazz DJed a large poetry event for his dad's birthday at the Brooklyn Museum. I produced the event, and we all shared the stage. We are still healing and growing closer, and that is a blessing.

I'm currently a single mom, happily raising my fantastic five-and-a-half-year-old son King Thomas. I've learned so much about love. Sometimes, I think my heart belongs on another planet, but I am fighting against the idea that "you don't have to love their kids."

In fact you must love them, and love your Baby Mamas. Our community has to get past Western ideas about love and raising children. Parenting is so fragile, and children should never be kept from love, even if it's not convenient. I have made an effort not to allow my grownup issues to influence who my son is allowed to love, and vice versa.

The great lesson I've learned from falling in love with men who have children is that I am a great mother. And that is an incredible gift. It's a gift not always easy to accept when opened, but it comes with a reward beyond my own imagination. My birth/earth/step-children are my ribbons, holding down my present, and fearlessly helping me to release the past.

> Love Is Not the Enemy.
> Love Is Not the Enemy.
> Love Is Not the Enemy.
> I promise.

—jessica Care moore

jessica Care moore is an internationally renowned poet/publisher/ activist/rock star/playwright/actor. She is a five-time Showtime at the Apollo *winner, was featured on hip-hop megastar Nas's album* Nastradamus, *and was a recurring star of Russell Simmons's HBO series* Def Poetry Jam. *Moore is the founder of Moore Black Press, which has published work by famed poets Saul Williams and Sharrif Simmons; Def Poetry Jam cofounder Danny Simmons; and NBA basketball player Etan Thomas, among others.*

CHAPTER 6

The Problem with Marriage

THE FIRST (AND SO FAR ONLY) TIME I GOT MARRIED WAS A disaster. A "youthful indiscretion." I was only 23 and afraid to be alone. A few years prior, I'd moved away from home for the first time since graduating college. I was always a family person. Even when I made friends, I usually saw them more as family. I tried to create a surrogate version of the family I'd left behind in St. Louis.

Trying this with an equally-young-but-controlling-and-confused new husband was a disaster. He was cruel and wasteful and rude. And I let myself be a doormat in order to keep the peace—until the peace was unbearable. I was giving in, but getting nothing in return. There were endless hoops to jump through, and then I'd still be told I'd failed.

So, against everything inside of me, we divorced. I fell into a deep depression over how I'd "wasted" my chance at forever happiness on someone who was incapable of going the distance. I believed marriage was something you only got one shot at, and I'd blown it. I hated myself for it long after I'd forgiven and forgotten him. Marriage had meant so much to me.

It took me a while to realize that despite all the bad ways people think about marriage—from a blind obsession with it to staunch opposition to it—secretly, it didn't mean that much to a significant minority of people. They just didn't feel all that comfortable admitting it.

A lot of people now are waiting longer to get married, or are deciding to never get married. There is a lot of talk in the news about how this "decline" of marriage is due to some dramatic loss of values, rather than acknowledging reality: Marriage is a social construct, and like all social constructs, it is prone to change according to the expectations, rules, and mores of a society at any given time. For a very long time, marriage was largely about property ties and birth-right—and often without a voice in the matter, women were part of both. It later evolved into a covenant between a man and a woman, and sometimes God, with marriage being of a higher purpose in a civilized world. Even still, women were still often viewed as property, and marriage was still a pretty good way to solidify various social and business ties.

When marriage is forced upon (or at least, expected of) functional members of society, it becomes a slog. Not everyone would choose it for themselves. Unhappy marriages are a product of our society, our various faiths, and our romantic expectations (or delusions), which tell us that marriage should be forever. Forever is a long time when you consider the whims of fickle human beings.

As soon as people argued for more control over how and why they married, what marriage signified began to change. What constitutes marriage in an agrarian society divided into different city-states cannot be the same kind of marriage that exists in a society where women are considered human beings with agency. Marriage defined by politics and transfers of wealth cannot be the same as marriage defined by love. Yet we in our modern, no-fault-divorce world still hold ourselves to the outdated concept of forever-and-ever-amen marriage.

This doesn't mean marriage is bad or wrong. In fact, I'm about as promarriage as any person you'd meet. I love the idea of marriage. I love actual marriage. I was married once, and when it failed, it scarred me in a way nothing else has. My parents will celebrate their fortieth anniversary this year, and I credit the health of their union as a crucial part of my own well-being and self-esteem. I think marriage could solve a lot of the problems people have, especially black people—to a certain extent. More on that later.

I want to discuss the problem with marriage, which is that we live in a world where one's success in life is still measured by whether or not he or she marries. We still live under the assumption that to never marry is a form of failure. We live in a world where all are expected to marry despite the fact that very few people are actually suited for the kind of marriage we glorify and write crappy love songs about.

What do I mean by this? Let me say this uncomfortable truth: If you are honest, truly honest with yourself, you already know if you're suited for marriage. And let's say you figured out a long time ago that you'd be bad at the forever-and-ever-amen brand of it. Yet you are still expected to marry because that is how success is measured, and you will fail at it because you are not the marrying kind. You will fail and grow to loathe yourself and pity your way of life. You will internalize all the angst and frustration that goes with trying to cram square pegs into round holes.

You are not alone. There is a plurality of people who suck at this version of marriage and always have. However, throughout history, there was no way out of marriage that wasn't grueling, deadly or complicated, because marriages were iron-clad contracts handed down by God and your parents and the legal system, just to make you miserable.

In my opinion, forever-and-ever-amen marriage requires a very specific personality type to succeed without intervention from punitive laws, threat of damnation, or the rejection of your family. But you only need two essential traits to be good at it: (1) you need to believe that family/community/God/whoever is more important than the individual, and (2) you have to be willing to compromise.

It sounds simple. And on the surface, this might not sound too bad either. You like your family. You're cool with your community. You're willing to compromise. "What do you mean I'm not good at that, Danielle? I could totally do that," you say.

Except you were born into modern Western society, where what is valued above all else is the individual self. Otherwise, we'd all still be living with our parents or just down the street from them, raising our kids alongside our siblings' children, raising barns, and calling ourselves Amish.

The United States glorifies and celebrates the triumph of the individual over society, nature, and government. Our heroes are "self-made" men and women. You are expected (and encouraged) to leave home at the advent of adulthood. You are encouraged to own a home, succeed in your chosen career, make lots of money, acquire things, and make a name for yourself—often all before you get married. In fact, we have extended the age range that we consider to be adolescence so people can have more than just high school to figure out who they are and to amass wealth and status. This means young adulthood has gone from ending at 14 to ending at 16 to ending at 18 to ending at 21 to where people still see themselves as "young" and "still growing" at 30.

The expansion of adolescence makes sense when you consider that we live much longer now and we have many more choices than those who came before us. We celebrate choices and freedoms and opportunities. We have turned our backs on the notions of arranged marriages, of marrying to forge community and monetary ties, of marrying out of respect for the church. No one does this anymore.

Now we marry for some loose notion of love and family, often half-thought out by people who aren't good at forever-and-ever-amen marriage, but who are still expected to take a crack at it.

If you were raised to celebrate the individual, and you spend your twenties "discovering yourself" and starting your career, by your mid-thirties, you have been on your own for so long that you may find it difficult to compromise. You are used to getting your way. You are used to having things the way you like them. Before, when people got married at 18 or 21, they didn't really have time to discover what they liked and disliked. They and their spouse sort of figured out these things as they went along.

If you have been single and on your own since 19, you've probably figured out whether you're a Democrat or a Republican, whether you prefer Downy fabric softener to Bounce, and whether you're a neat person or a slob. You have the spice rack just the way you like it. The junk in your junk drawer is your junk, and you don't care if the bathroom gets a little cruddy, because it's just *your* dead flakes of skin and toenails and dust and hair and toothpaste gunk. And you're immune to your own grossness.

Someone else's grossness may turn you into a cleaning Nazi. And that's just the small stuff. We haven't even gotten into how you view your faith (or whether you have one or not); how you view your sexual needs; and how you view your work habits, money habits, and dietary needs.

Instead of two dumb kids learning how to be grownups together, marriages are now forged between two people who have already mastered their individual lives but are foisted into a world that is nothing but constant negotiations over everything from retirement savings to what religion to raise the children to what brand of toilet cleaner to buy. And you're already used to getting your way, because for decades you only had you to care for. And you live in the United States and were raised in a society that celebrates the individual over family, community, and church.

Yet understanding these attributes is necessary in order to have a marriage that lasts 40 to 50 years. And even if you do possess those two things, there is yet another caveat: You have to marry someone who *also* possesses those two traits.

My parents, for all their differences, have largely stayed married for 40 years because of these traits. While they care about their own individual wants and needs, my mother and father define themselves by their relationships with their family and their community. It may not always look that way to the naked eye, but if you talk to them long enough, you will find that although they have their own selfish tendencies, fundamentally they judge themselves by how well they have performed their roles as daughter/sister/aunt/mother and son/brother/uncle/father.

To my mother, family was everything. She adores her large but extremely interconnected Southern family. She is closest to and bonded with those who share her bloodline. She has lived her life in a moral way, defined by her relationships with and love for her family. When she grows sad or depressed, it is because she wonders whether she has been a "good enough" wife or mother. When she is resentful, it's because she wonders if she took enough time for herself, as she has lived unselfishly at the expense of her own wants. My father is very similar in that he prides himself on being a provider. Being able to take care of his wife, mother-in-law, and daughters is what makes him feel he has lived a good life.

That's not to say they didn't have their own personal indulgences: My father loves TV, and my mother is obsessively clean. This is why the second component, being willing to engage in endless negotiation and compromise, is so important.

My father knows it is illogical to live in a home and expect that nothing will ever get messed up. Yet he also knows it is pointless to fight with my fastidiously clean mother about it. Happiness means accepting that my mother will put rugs under all the couches and chairs, own about five different versions of the same vacuum cleaner, and yell at him at for leaving crumbs on the kitchen counter. Why would he put up with this? Because to him, it is worth it.

His reward for listening to my mother complain about the billionth time he tracked grass in the house after mowing the lawn is that he gets to live in a house where if he drops food on the floor, he can pick it right up and continue eating it because there has not been any real accumulation of dirt in the house since it was built. He doesn't have to wash dishes or do laundry. There's no such thing as running out of something. He has compromised, and to this day continues to negotiate with my mother and her obsession with cleanliness.

In turn, my dad watches an obscene amount of sports-related television—probably more than most men. My mother is the ultimate sports widow, as she never has an off-season. My father loves it all, from NASCAR to major-league baseball. Tennis, boxing, most Olympic sports, and horse racing are all of great fascination to him. He can recall many details and greatly enjoys conversations about these details. His love of sports means that at times, my father is simply not available. Phone calls made during basketball games get cut short. Family outings are planned around the football season schedule. A Sunday conversation about anything other than the spread is almost unheard of.

And my mother doesn't like sports. Maybe she once enjoyed them occasionally, but after years of exposure to every sport in the world, she has grown to truly dislike them and my father's monopolization of the TV to watch them. My mother loathes the TV except for those moments when (1) it's the news or (2) *In the Heat of the Night* (or something similar) is on.

The rest of the time, my mother would actually prefer that the TV be turned off. Instead, she'd rather listen to some really raunchy blues or soul or some uplifting gospel. And things have only gotten worse since my father retired, as now the TV is on from 5 a.m. until late in the evening most days. And it is almost always turned to sports. When not on sports, it's on ESPN Sports Zone. It's been 40 years of this.

Why hasn't my mother waged a war for the remote, you ask? Because TV is my father's reward for being an excellent husband and provider. My mother has never had to work outside the home during her marriage to my father, but my father often worked long hours in a career he found both rewarding and very draining. Where another man may have unwound from work by beating up his wife, getting drunk, or engaging in multiple affairs, my father preferred to watch TV and eat ice cream. While this did nothing for his waistline, it did keep the peace. Instead of growling at all of us from the pressures of being the sole breadwinner, he just watched sports and got all his therapy via Magic Johnson doing a baby sky-hook on the Celtics.

So even in retirement, my mother lets my father have the remote in relative peace and grumbles only to me about how annoying it is when he spends an entire weekend watching golf as she falls asleep from boredom.

Although these examples may seem small to you, these tradeoffs exist in every form and at every level of my parents' marriage. Every day together is a negotiation, both big and small: whether or not my sisters and I would be raised Baptist over Methodist, whether we would vacation at my grandmother's house or some other locale, whether they would invest in savings bonds or an IRA, what schools we would attend, whether we would stay in St. Louis or move, what kind of home they would buy, and who would get the big piece of chicken (answer: never my mother).

Self-sacrifice. The willingness to constantly compromise. These are the things that will determine the success of your forever-and-ever-amen marriage. Not if he's hot or if she's rich. Nope. It will be whether you have the will or desire to put someone else's needs ahead of your own and actually take pride in it. And you both have to have these traits, especially in a modern marriage, because without them, divorce is almost inevitable.

I was built for forever-and-ever-amen marriage. It's what I was raised on. I have a keen understanding of the constant negotiation and self-sacrifice involved, and I tend to view family as more important than the individual. This does not mean my view of marriage is right for everyone, or that it is the better view.

On the contrary, I'd argue my view is actually ill-suited and retrograde for what today's marriage market truly is: a celebration of the serial monogamist. Serial monogamy—the good kind, not the kind you throw out as an excuse for your constant infidelity—is the style of marriage that actually suits most people. It is the belief that marriage is for a reason and season, and when either or both have passed, the marriage should end. The reason this actually works better for many people is because of one particular complication that comes with long-term, decades-spanning commitment: You're going to change.

I hate to tell you all this, but you're going to get old. As you get old, what you need and want will change. At 21, maybe you need excitement and adventure. At 25, maybe you need beauty and strength. At 30, maybe you need hot sex mixed with easygoing companionship. At 40, maybe you need stability and predictability. After 50, maybe you need someone who was going to make sure you didn't die in your sleep of shit no one dies of anymore. The type of person you fall in love or lust with at 21 and end up marrying might not make that great of a spouse at 35.

Now, this isn't guaranteed. There is always a chance that the person you enjoyed screwing like rabbits with in your twenties and thirties will also be the person you enjoy talking to and quietly depending on in your forties, fifties, and sixties. But often what we find is that who you are at 21 is not who you are at 41. You've changed, which means the relationship, and what you need out of it, will change. And not always for the better.

When Al Gore and his longtime wife Tipper broke up, many were shocked. They'd made it to 40 years. "Why now?" some wondered. As the primary witness to my parents' marriage, I can easily understand how you could make it to 40 years and go, "Deuces, I'd rather die alone."

Marriage is hard. Not just superficially, but actually *hard* hard. As in, if it doesn't work out with this one person, you might not ever want to try this shit again. You might think no one else is worth it once you know what kind of compromise and work it actually entails. You might just want your life back after devoting the last 40 years of it to someone.

People change. And in 40 years, you may discover that the free-hearted, happy-go-lucky, clueless, romantic guy you married grew up to be a conflicted, bitter, crabby old man. Maybe (and this is a big maybe) valuing the community over the individual and your willingness to compromise will pull you through. Even a forever-and-ever-amen marriage, however, can be done in by discovering the person you loved is now someone else entirely due to the passing of time.

Retirement is especially hard, as having a career or children can distract a married couple for *decades* from the actual issues in their marriage. But once you're both home, alone, staring at each other, you may discover that things are not as easy as you'd thought they would be, since the last time it was just the two of you, you were in your late twenties. This is why serial monogamy, a series of commitments (or even marriages) that take place over a lifetime, may actually work better for some people.

This concept of a soul mate that we are fed, the idea that there is only one person in the world meant for us—that's a terrifying concept. It gives the impression that we only have one shot, and if we miss it, there's no way to ever feel real love or happiness again. We don't view friendships that way. We don't think there's only one shot at finding a best friend, and if we blow it, we'll never find that "true friend." That's ridiculous. That's like believing you only have enough love for one child and might not love your second or third child enough.

There is no real limit on love. It's an endless reservoir. You won't run out. Love isn't finite. It's more like the mythological phoenix that lives and dies and lives again. You can love many people in many different ways. You can meet the love of your life for your twenties and then meet a different love of your life who is perfect for your thirties or forties or fifties or your twilight years. If you don't find romantic contentment until you are 57, is it somehow worth less than if you had found it at 27? There's what's right and there's what's right now, and I believe we shouldn't feel bad if we've found either at any given time.

The implications of serial monogamy only sound frightening if you think of breakups and divorce as shameful. That's a mentality people should fight at all costs. But if you have no problem with divorce, if you understand that love can end and people can change, why mock or dismiss those who treat life as an endless exploration, sometimes alone and sometimes with a partner? It can be just as beautiful as you-and-me-against-the-world-forever-and-ever-amen, just like how you still fondly remember your childhood best friend, the frat brother or sorority sister you were closest to in college, your best friend from the office, and the close friend you made while doing charity work. Sometimes an end isn't failure, but simply an end.

If we are honest about who we are and what we want, we can find romantic success in that honesty. If we stop penalizing ourselves for not fulfilling some imaginary, trumped-up ideal that was invented to get women to enter contractual marriages where they were treated as property, and instead celebrate each other with honesty and respect, we may find love far more rewarding.

In my life, I have truly loved only two men. With one of them, the love ended, and I don't feel it anymore. The other is a close and dear friend. And as I am someone built for the long term, so is our friendship. I don't have many regrets, other than the fact that my propensity to be so serious in love and life has meant that I often spend a lot of time single and alone. I understand the value and complications of coupling up and marriage, so I miss out on some of the fun that others experience of just coming together and seeing what happens. But sometimes I envy those times and wish I had more of them. I wish that I could turn off the tape in my head that can see that he might be nice for right now, but that a relationship makes little to no sense in the long term, when nothing is left but words, nostalgia, and (ideally) warm memories.

My father's eyes still light up when he remembers the thrill of first falling in love with my mother. And he enjoys looking at old pictures of the two of them, young and fit, wearing matching dashikis my mother had made with her sewing machine, the whole world ahead of them. They sit on the couch next to each other going through these albums and remembering their four decades together. They had a romantic love once, but what exists now has gone beyond the passion and excitement and charm and beauty of youth and has given way to a bond that has seen them through illness, death, disappointment, and malaise.

In the end, they appreciate each other and are a team. And their bond means more than the individual. And that neither will probably never marry again if it doesn't work out. Because to go through something like this with anyone else sounds like a nightmare.

My grandmother told me once after my grandpa died that one man in one lifetime was enough for her. They were together almost 60 years, since she was 16. When we were younger, she constantly told us to enjoy our youth, have fun, and be adventurous, because she sacrificed her youth and individuality at the altar of marriage and family. And while she has known nothing else but marriage, she also knows that you are only young once, and maybe it wouldn't be such a bad thing for a girl to grow up and find herself and her own way before gaining a husband and putting his needs before her own.

Yet we envy what she had, despite the fact that she openly admits she would have done it differently and would have never done it again with any other man. It's like the 1976 song by Candi Staton seeking to warn young lovers about the mistakes of their parents: "What's the sense in sharing, this one and only life?"

Of course, these visions come from older eyes looking back at what was lost and feeling regret over what could or should have happened, often at the expense of all the wonderful things that *did* happen. Maybe they would have done something differently, but look at what would have been lost if they had? Every choice reverberates with consequences seen and unforeseen.

What I'm suggesting though—for all sides of the marriage divide—is that we abandon the Disney fiction of Happily Ever After and create realistic expectations for what marriage means to us as individuals and as a community. We will never go back to the fairy tale that once was, because we left that model for a reason. We need to embrace the wants and desires of who we choose might change with age and time.

We cannot blame marriage. It is not marriage's fault we fail at it. Our own unrealistic expectations and our rejection of what is at the core of ourselves are to blame. We feel that we are different, that we want to choose differently. We don't agree with what has always been done, but we fear rejection for having these thoughts and feelings. However, embracing these thoughts is the only way to save marriage.

Marriage by threat and individualism at the cost of society are extreme choices. There has to be a balance, where those who are not suited for marriage are respected for their decision and not told to put on a mask of fidelity and inspire misery in themselves and others. And we cannot have a world where those who see the benefit of long-term partnering are accused of being paternalistic, sexist, old-fashioned, antiquated, or pathetic. There is no morally right or wrong choice between marrying for forever and coupling for a while before moving on. What's right is being honest in our intentions. What's wrong is being covert, wishing to imperson-ate the skin of a monogamous person in order to win favor with others.

It's time for serial monogamy to come out of the closet and it is time for us to rethink what family means, what forever means, and what friendship means. Close bonds are what tie us together, but de-sire and lies tear us apart. If we are to come together with any success, we must start with honesty and declare who we are without shame. Starting with honesty means we can better build our relationships and families without the sense that we have failed because we didn't do something we were never suited for in the first place.

Stop trying to force what never came natural. Declare who you are and embrace it. My name is Danielle Belton, and I will love you forever, but if you're not capable of the same, maybe I'll love you from a distance. It's only fair to both of us.

—**Danielle Belton**

Danielle C. Belton was born and raised St. Louis, Missouri, on a healthy diet of news programming, pop culture, black history, and snark. Belton is best known for her pop-culture-meets-politics blog, The Black Snob, through which she examines the irreverent side of American life. Less than two years after its inception, the blog has a readership of over two million, including the likes of political junkies, journalists, fellow bloggers, political pundits, authors, academics, legislators and political strategists. Belton has earned widespread critical acclaim, and her work has appeared in the New York Times, Time *magazine, the* Observer *(UK), the* Daily Beast, *and on NPR. Belton has also been a featured guest on CNN, ABC's* Nightline *and* Good Morning America, *NBC's* Today Show, *and MSNBC's* The Last Word with Lawrence O'Donnell. *Belton also makes regular appearances on PBS's* To the Contrary with Bonnie Erbe *and NPR's* Tell Me More. *Currently she is a writer for* Don't Sleep! *hosted by T.J. Holmes and produced by Mad Cow Productions.*

CHAPTER 7

Love Is Not Enough

LOVE IS NOT ENOUGH. THAT'S WHAT I LEARNED FROM
marriage. Five years of marriage. Two separations and six
different moves in and out of each other's lives to find freedom. An eternity's worth of experiences and lessons.

I could blame society for socializing me to want a wedding.
Raised by Barbie and Ken, I dreamed of a dashing prince taking my
hand and walking me down the aisle. I remember perusing the pages
of *Essence* magazine, searching for the perfect wedding dress. I was
only 12.

I could blame TV for my outlook on matrimony—*The Cosby
Show*, to be exact. The Huxtables had the perfect setup: He was a
doctor and she a lawyer. They had a million-dollar brownstone,
beautiful children with minor problems, a grandma and grandpa
who made frequent visits, and a marriage without arguments. It was
a fantasy that I and most other '80s babies aspired to. But it was a
one-sided representation of marriage, highlighting all of the positives
and benefits while masking the reality of imminent communication
breakdowns and beefs. *The Cosby Show* showed us the peaks of Happily Ever After, but neglected the hurtful valleys and how to climb
out of them.

I could blame statistics for my slim odds at having a successful
union: It is often reported that around 70 percent of African-American households are headed by a single parent. Usually it's Mom, and
Dad is nowhere to be found.

I could go back to the '60s and point a finger at J. Edgar Hoover,
who, conspiracy theorists say, set up the welfare system to break
down the black family and take the father out of the home.

I could blame my upbringing, because children learn by watching. A single-parent household often brings up children who don't

know how to deal with the opposite sex or how to love, fight, communicate, or make up without breaking up. I envy those who had an opportunity to see a man and woman in both love and war, a couple who stuck it out through thick and thin, staying together until the bitter end. I, like many of my African-American peers, didn't grow up seeing marriages. And now some of us contribute to the incredibly high divorce rate in the United States of America. These are disappointing, depressing statistics that make me and many of my fellow Generation Xers shy away from matrimony. We are now contemplating the possibility of having a life partner instead of a legally documented union.

I could blame the idiot who came up with the idea that "opposites attract." Yeah, it's absolutely true, but opposites don't last. Take a look at your circle, the friendships that bonded back in high school or college. If they've passed the decade mark, it's likely because you have more in common than not. Your outlooks on life, love, and how to deal with them are often the same. We are more like our closest friends than not, as having a common bond cements a lifelong foundation together. It's the differences that pull us apart.

Ultimately, I blame myself for the breakdown of my marriage. A woman is blessed with the power of intuition. Our sixth sense tells us when to go, but we often ignore it, suppressing the voice in our heads that's whispering warnings. Before jumping the broom, I brushed away the gentle tickles on my earlobe that made my neck itch and twitch with warnings. "Don't do it, Raqiyah," the angels said. "Don't get married." Their pleading got progressively louder during my nine-month rush down the aisle.

Our fights stemmed from having different backgrounds and experiences:

- **Politics:** I voted. He didn't, based on a lackadaisical 'hood logic that the system can't and won't ever change, no matter how many times we vote. I likened that outlook to shitting on the graves of ancestors who fought and died to win coloreds their rights.
- **God:** I believe in God, and he didn't. An atheist to the core. He spoke of man-made myths and rewritings of the Bible.

I believed that "the family that prays together stays together," wanting to bless our meals and head to church on the occasional Sunday morning.

- **Money:** I was the super saver, making the most bread.
- **Family:** I was the one who worked to attend all family functions and reunions. He resented his kin, preferring to lie in bed while I trekked to Jersey with his son to see my people.
- **Education:** I was college-educated and from the suburbs. He was a reformed thug from the Bronx, a high-school dropout with a GED who pursued a secondary education for a semester before distractions and financial issues forced him to leave.

Because of these differences, I subconsciously believed that I was smarter, savvier, and more sophisticated, which resulted in my taking over. I made all of the plans and decisions pertaining to the relationship. The result: My respect for him vanished.

This is all hindsight-is-20/20 reflection, of course. Because at the time, early on, and even when we wed, I strongly believed that love was all we needed. He and I laughed, took long walks, and talked of dreams and wants. Yes, our ideals were polar opposites. But I believed and romanticized that opposites attract. It was innocent and beautiful. I could teach and show him things. We could live on an island, hold hands all day, snuggle, and be okay—alone, broke, and without a prayer, thought, or need for anyone else.

Today, in my post-divorce clarity, reality prevails. Society, TV, and all the messages we receive tell us that love is enough. And yes, it should be. But it is not. Love, in its purest form, is more like a baby. Pittering. Pattering. Innocent. Untouched. It wants to be held, cuddled, and kissed. But as it matures, it morphs into a child with a new toy. And the intrigue often wears off. The magic fades. Everything else comes into focus, the things that matter most in maintaining matrimonial longevity: politics. God. Money. Family values. Upbringing. Education. These all need to mesh and be on the same page for a lasting, healthy relationship. We keep our longtime friends because we have more in common with them. We see eye to eye and sympathize with each other even when we're miles apart.

So what did I learn from marriage? Marry your best friend. Because when the love gets dusty, and the innocent, twinkling magic fades, you can look into your partner's eyes and still see a homey. You'll joke about the bullshit, talk about it, laugh it off, and ultimately enjoy one another day by day. Because that's what friends are for—marriage and more.

—Raqiyah Mays

A former staff member of Vibe *magazine, Raqiyah Mays has written for the Associated Press,* Essence, Billboard, *and MSNBC's theGrio.com, to name a few. Mays produced radio shows for Grandmaster Flash before going on to host her own shows on New York City's Hot 97 and 98.7 Kiss FM, where she also co-hosted a morning show with D.L. Hughley.*

Mays has performed Off-Broadway and in a slew of independent films. She has made appearances as a pundit and cultural expert on FOX News, MTV, Fuse, and VH1, which in 2009 named her a "Future Leader of Black History." Mays currently coordinates nonprofit fundraisers, art receptions, and assorted affairs for film through her event planning company, Broadway Night Out.

CHAPTER 8

The Art of Attachment

"Therefore shall a man 'leave' his father and his mother, and shall 'cleave' unto his wife: and they shall be one flesh."

—Genesis 2:24

FOR YEARS, I'VE HEARD THE "LEAVE AND CLEAVE" SCRIPTURE, but until recently I didn't see the irony of it. "Leave" assumes you were once connected to something or someone in the first place. But what if you never were? What if, as a child, you were never appropriately attached to your parents? Then what? How do you leave where you've never been, and cleave (that is, adhere or cling) to a wife? Now that is the question.

As many black families strive to deal with single-parent homes and appropriate relationship behavior, "modeling" has become a frequent topic of conversation. Is the concept of attachment even considered in that dialogue? We have too many couples and families who never make a long-term commitment, and too many weddings that end in painful divorce, all because attachment is not getting the attention it deserves. As a result, vast numbers of men try to build connections together but don't know how, and they don't know what being connected feels like. They don't feel worthy of it. Beneath their public façades lie insecurities and the self-sabotaging behaviors that ruin relationships.

If you see people as disposable, and you feel like you can't let anyone see your true self, you might do things to destroy your relationships (e.g., cheat, lie, deceive) because you feel that the "real" you will never be truly accepted. The black community can ill afford to continue lumping all of these detached and "walking wounded" behaviors into some sort or "normal" or "man thing" category. None of us are off the hook, and as a community we must adopt new models as part of our "real man" and "fully grown man" criteria.

Black men need to reshape how they see themselves ("I am enough" instead of "I am inadequate"), change their attitudes ("I am blessed" instead of "I am doomed"), and embrace the possibility that real love can exist ("She loves me for me" instead of "She'll end up leaving anyway"). A change in self-perception is in order for our brothers to fully connect with those who seek to love them.

Recently, I experienced a genuine "aha!" moment when I took part in celebrating my goddaughter's 5th birthday party. Of course, she was super excited, and nothing could mess with her special day. However, a short walk outside resulted in a fall that did just that. Instantly, tears fell as she reached for her parents and they reached for her. On the surface, it was no big deal, but it all seemed to move in slow motion.

There I was, witnessing firsthand as a little girl tested the empathy, compassion, and condition of her parents' love. Without hesitation, they tag teamed to let her know she was okay; it wasn't the end of the world; and most importantly, there was more fun in store for her. Her parents weren't just modeling a healthy male/female relationship; they were also reinforcing their family connection. They were teaching her proper attachment through which she could confirm her own identity and self-worth. Together, they were laying the groundwork that will prepare her to be cleaved to, and become one with, someone in the future.

In that moment with my godchild, it all clicked. Too many black boys don't experience this positive parental attachment, which becomes an issue when they become adults. They feel disconnected, numb, unloved, and inadequate, all of which fosters a lack of intimacy with their partners. Appropriate childhood attachment reinforces the value of connection, trust, and vulnerability as necessary aspects of the human experience. When you learn that your parents will love you no matter what, you lose the need to prove you're loved, because internally, you already know it to be true. That truth further fosters a sense of worth and belonging.

As a community, it's our collective job to make it easier for detached men to heal. We must encourage our men to accept who they are and be more open to hope in their lives. Parents must show our young male children love and provide them with stability and a view of the world that inspires them with confidence. Our sons need to trust our decisions, our intentions, and our ability to keep promises. Attachment is important to this development of trust that, in turn, is critical to relationships.

Too many women in our community are married but not properly attached because their men never cleaved. Although attachment does not make for a perfect life or a perfect marriage, it can make a difference. It's time for black men to accept their role in the current state of their relationships with the women in their lives.

Black men can make the difference. They can be the ones who declare war on their wounds and use the insight to gain the control to change their lives. This is a journey that black men not only can embrace, but also can lead wholeheartedly.

—Nicole LaBeach

Dr. Nicole LaBeach, aka Dr. Nicole, is a success strategist who empowers the new generation to get in the driver's seat of their own lives and strive for their personal best. Radio personalities from Steve Harvey to Tom Joyner have shared LaBeach's expertise with their listeners. As CEO of Volition Enterprises, Inc., a premiere personal and professional development firm, she has spent over 15 years working with Fortune 500 companies, as well as faith-based and entertainment clientele. LaBeach is the new voice for a new generation. She hosts the weekly Blog Talk Radio program The Dr. Nicole Show. *Learn more about her at www.askdrnicole.com.*

CHAPTER 9

Patience, Sacrifice, and Marriage

I THINK A LOT OF MY ATTITUDES ABOUT RELATIONSHIPS WERE subconsciously filtered into my psyche from my mother. My parents, Fred and Charcle Lee Payne, had me first. My sister, Scherrie, came along a year and a half later. Unfortunately, the marriage did not last. My mother divorced my father when I was three and a half years old because she discovered he was being unfaithful. She found it unforgivable.

I know that for some people, cheating is unforgivable, and it breaks their connection to their partner. My mother always vilified my father, but she also made sure that my sister and I had a relationship with him and his family. Her feelings about men and relationships were very complicated, and I think she passed that down to me. When I get into a relationship with someone, I always become suspicious.

I am single right now, but in 1976 I married the R&B singer Gregory Abbott. When we first met, I thought he was the perfect mate for me and that our relationship would last forever. However, our marriage only lasted two years. When I met Gregory, he was a graduate student at Stanford University working on his PhD. He was not working in the music business. I don't know what it is, but after a person goes through the ceremony and signs the marriage license, and everything settles down—that's when the real person comes out.

I think our marriage could have worked if I had tried harder. In retrospect, I can now say that maybe I was the one who wasn't giving him the time and space to grow into the person that he needed to be. But instead, I found some of his impulses annoying. Eventually, I grew to dislike him, but maybe I just couldn't accept criticism from him. What I now know is that if I had been more tolerant, our relationship would have lasted longer.

A woman's thriving career can be challenging to a relationship. A man's ego is very fragile, and unless a woman is willing to buckle down and work hard at keeping her man's ego propped up, there can be problems. A man will become resentful of a woman who earns more money than he does. He thinks of it as if she is better than him. He wants her to be his woman, and he wants to be the man and the breadwinner. It really does get down to who is "the man."

I can't help anyone find a mate. That has to happen by the will of God. I can say that once you find someone, it's best to take your time and go slow. My mother used to always say, "Anything that comes easy, goes easy…"

There is so much going on now that didn't exist when I was coming up. Nowadays, morals are much more relaxed, and young people are exposed to a lot more than they were 30 or 40 years ago. I think they are being exposed too early now. From what I've observed, young women today are a lot more willing to lose their virginity at an early age, and I think we have to slow that down.

When it comes to keeping a marriage together, I think it all boils down to how much patience you are willing to have and how much you can tolerate. Too often, the moment that something goes wrong, everyone wants to throw the towel in and walk away. For a relationship to last, people need to understand the power of patience, understanding, and love. People don't want to admit that their mates aren't perfect, or that they have faults as well. But it's true, so you must have patience to work through it all. It's important for couples to come to some sort of resolution or agreement, and their love must outweigh whatever faults either individual brings to the relationship. You have to be willing to sacrifice to make it work.

I don't think there is a golden rule about successful relationships. Sometimes it's just the luck of the draw. I personally haven't been lucky in relationships, but I've learned that despite the challenges, you must be willing to overcome and be willing to sacrifice in order for things to work. It's important to follow your heart, but it's equally important to find a partner with whom you have a lot in common, including the same spiritual beliefs. Finally, you must be open to communication and always maintain respect for one another.

—**Freda Payne**

Freda Payne is an internationally acclaimed singer and actress best known for her hit singles "Band of Gold" and "Bring the Boys Home." An entertainment veteran, Payne has performed on Broadway, on television, and in films. Visit her website at www.fredapayne.com.

CHAPTER 10

Reflections from a Realistic Romantic

LIKE BILLIONS OF OTHERS IN THIS WORLD, MY PERCEPTION OF love was influenced by fairy tales, music, cinema, literature, television shows, religious teachings, and commercials from eHarmony and Match.com. I believed in the marriage vows of "happily ever after, 'till death do us part"—that is, until recently. I had an epiphany: As a grown woman who still hasn't met "the one," I needed to do some serious introspection about relationships. I took some time to engage in deep reflection about my previous intimate involvements and why they didn't prevail. Part of why I did this was to learn from the past so my future relationships could be healthy and sustainable.

Flash back to some of your past romantic relationships: Can you identify commonalities that led to their ultimate demise? Do you construct or destruct your love foundations? What kind of lover are you? One of my best friends calls himself a hopeful romantic. I commend him, but after experiencing the ups, downs, and turnarounds of love, I would describe myself as more of a realistic romantic.

First, let me acknowledge that while I am a loving, giving, spirited woman, I am also a flawed, menopausal, Afro-Rican female subject to mood swings who sometimes carries a trunk's worth of emotional baggage full of the pain of past disappointments. Whew. With that said, I'll admit to having contributed to the unraveling of a few significant relationships with men I loved (and with whom I had hoped to cross the finish line). I've accepted my culpability, and I've started to seriously examine not just my own unsuccessful situations, but also the crumbled relationships of my friends, family, and associates. This self-scrutiny helped me realize that I am a realistic romantic. How can we become less caught up in fantasy and fairy tale love, and instead root ourselves in real deal ways to cultivate substantive romantic relationships?

As I pondered various scenarios, it dawned on me that folks put their best forward when they begin dating someone new. People try so hard to hide their flaws. Some will ignore their partner's flaws because "love is blind," or the sex is super-duper good, or maybe they just don't want to be alone; whatever the case, they overlook traits that can become major issues as the relationship progresses. Furthermore, they aren't always forthcoming about their true feelings. Case in point: A player meets a lady and tells her he isn't ready or interested in a committed relationship. The woman will tell him that it's cool, but she proceeds with an ulterior motive. In the front of her mind, she is out to claim her man, change his mind, and be his one and only. People, please keep it real. If you are honest about what you want, don't want, will accept, and won't accept, you can avert conflicts and eventual breakups.

I recently made a joke to a girlfriend recovering from an abusive relationship who has dived into the deep end of the dating pool. I told her that perhaps before dating anyone new, she should give him sodium pentothal (truth serum) and a polygraph (lie detector) test, secure his medical and credit reports, and check for a criminal record. I said this in jest, but the more I thought about it, the more I felt this notion wasn't so far-fetched. Maybe I should set up an agency! Seriously, not only are many people deceptive in the beginning of relationships, but these lies (both little and big) erode the trust between partners, which leads to alienation.

What can one do to prolong a healthy love connection? I think that people should receive professional and/or spiritual counseling in the beginning of their love journey. How about a test similar to getting a driver's license? It could assess how compatible you and your partner are when it comes to conflict resolution, money management, sharing space together, values, and more. I would recommend periodic written evaluations of one another (like performance reviews at work), getting tune-ups (like we do with our vehicles), and constantly dedicating special energy to the improvement, vitality, and passion of our romantic relationships to avoid becoming part of the failure rate.

My mother's parents stayed married until death parted them. They struggled, prevailed against challenges, had six children, and remained loving partners for well over 50 years. Relationships these days seem to be rather transitory. We live in a get-it-right-away, rapid-pace society. Fast food joints, emails, texts, Twitter, IMs... we are accustomed to quick. What happened to people committing to one another through thick and thin, richer or poorer, sickness and health? Perhaps we should ask Britney Spears, whose first marriage, a Las Vegas quickie, ended after 72 hours. How about Kim Kardashian, who filed for divorce from Kris Humphries after a little over two months of marriage? Their shelf life was 72 days! I think it is high time for us to take our involvements more seriously, aim for conflict resolution, become more loving, and create lasting connections.

After experiencing the ups, downs, and turnarounds of love, I now know that I am a realistic romantic with a more sensible perspective. Mind you, I don't have all the answers, but I've addressed some of my questions. I am more realistic about the amount of work necessary to make a relationship thrive, and I can see things with greater clarity. While I know my man is on this planet somewhere, and someday I will meet him, in the meantime I am working on fixing things that I *know* are wrong with me. I think we should all be more pragmatic about our intimate involvements. With a healthy dose of self-love and sincerity, and a critical analysis of our past and present relationships, maybe we can ensure greater success in our present and future loves!

—Dyana Williams

Dyana Williams is a seasoned, award-winning broadcaster who has appeared on TV One's "Unsung" music documentary series. She is also the CEO and celebrity strategist for Influence Entertainment. The founder of the International Association of African American Music Foundation, Williams helped to establish June as Black Music Month with Rock and Roll Hall of Fame inductee Kenny Gamble. She is the mother of three incredible individuals, a lover of life, and a realistic romantic!